PRAISE FOR GOOGLE BOMB

"*Google Bomb* is a great book! The Constitution protects free speech, but slander is not free speech. Only cowards use slander as a means of expression; we should be able to know who the cowards of this world are and hold them accountable, and *Google Bomb* helps readers do that."

—Senator Walter G. "Skip" Campbell Jr.

"I haven't been this affected by a book in a long time. I went from a shaking rage to knots in my stomach to tears and finally to cheers. What happened to Sue could happen to any of us, and *Google Bomb's* practical guidance makes this a highly profound and useful book that the world needs to read."

—Michele Borba, Ed.D., parenting expert, author of
The Big Book of Parenting Solutions, and _Today Show_ contributor

"The Internet is a wonderful informational tool with the focus being on *informational*—not *character assassination*, which is cyber bullying. As a result of Sue Scheff's being cyber bullied, *Google Bomb* has been written to educate people about the Internet, cyber bullying, and the horrifying effects that cyber bullying can have on a person. Some children are so tormented that they use suicide as an alternative to ease their pain. There are some adults whose lives have been turned upside down and businesses that have faced financial ruin. *Google Bomb* offers solutions to virtual threats and character assassinations and is a wake-up call as to why we need tough legislation to protect the inno-cent—whether they be children, adults, or businesses. Bravo to Sue Scheff and John W. Dozier Jr. for writing this much-needed book."

—Ross Ellis, founder and chief executive officer,
Love Our Children USA

"The Internet can be a wonderful resource for adults and students alike. But as Sue Scheff's story illustrates, it can also be the perfect platform for a bully. Par-ents need to teach their kids to be safe online, just as they teach them to be safe in the "real" world, and *Google Bomb* offers a game plan that even a techno-phobe can execute. A must read for anyone who's ever posted their name on the Internet, but especially for those whose kids are doing so every day."

—Danielle Wood, editor-in-chief, education.com

"*Google Bomb* is an instructive and timely book that will only become increasingly relevant as our laws catch up to the realities of today's evolving technology. Sue's triumph over her attacker underscores the principle that there is no constitutionally protected right to defame others online."

—Fatima R. Fahmy, attorney-at-law

Google™
B🖤MB

John W. Dozier Jr.
and Sue Scheff

Health Communications, Inc.
Deerfield Beach, Florida

www.hcibooks.com

Library of Congress Cataloging-in-Publication Data

Dozier, John W.
    Google bomb : the untold story of the $11.3m verdict that changed the way
we use the Internet / by John W. Dozier, Jr. and Sue Scheff.
       p. cm.
    Includes index.
    ISBN-13: 978-0-7573-1415-5
    ISBN-10: 0-7573-1415-5
       1. Google (Firm)   2. Internet industry—United States.   3. Internet searching.
4. Information society.   I. Scheff, Sue.   II. Title.
    HD9696.8.U64G6636 2009
    338.7'6102504—dc22

                                                                            2009025598

Publisher: Health Communications, Inc.
           3201 S.W. 15th Street
           Deerfield Beach, FL 33442–8190

Cover photo © Media Bakery, © Rubberball
Cover design by Larissa Hise Henoch
Interior design and formatting by Lawna Patterson Oldfield

CONTENTS

ACKNOWLEDGMENTS FROM JOHN DOZIER JR.

When I received a call about doing a book on online defamation in the spring of 2008, I recalled a lunch seven years earlier. A good friend had encouraged me to write "the book" on the law of the web. I was fresh off a ride on the Internet bubble of the late 1990s, having founded a venture-backed e-commerce company and anxious to get back to being a trial lawyer. Not enough time, I thought, but in retrospect that was just an excuse to put off for tomorrow what did not at the time seem necessary.

By the spring of 2008, things had changed. That call made me realize that writing about what I knew was not only necessary, but essential. And so it is. I want to thank Sue Scheff for having the courage to write her story. She won't tell you how trying and painful it was recalling the nastiness. She had the courage and conviction to move this project forward even knowing that the worst for her may be yet to come because of it.

Michele Matrisciani has been the driving force in so enthusiastically ushering this project through HCI, our publisher. Her vision, foresight, and understanding have been exceptional, and Michele was willing to let me do it my way. The entire family at HCI has been impressively supportive and professional, and for that I express my deep and sincere appreciation.

This book would not have been written had not a well-regarded author set aside her time to support, cajole, and manage both Sue and me. She pulled the strings, focused the thoughts, spotted the holes, and led this effort in a way that made my writing far easier. Olivia, words cannot express the contribution you have made. You are a consummate professional in every sense of the word and someone I will hold in high esteem even when the Google Bombs are dropping all over me!

I wrote my portion of this book personally and I am responsible for any inaccuracies or errors. My informal editing team of Lisa Casey, Don Morris, Cameron Gilbert, and Nick Moraites provided excellent suggestions and feedback. Victoria Lawson and Lisa were always ready, willing, and able to deal with the marketing and public relations aspects of writing this book as I ran the Dozier Internet Law firm and then went home and wrote each night for months. Each of you contributed mightily to my ability to undertake this project.

On a personal note, I owe a debt of gratitude to Katrina Dozier for finding the time to deal with many of the everyday challenges of raising two teenagers. To my two sons, John III and Justin, thank you for understanding that Dad really, really needed to do something important every night for what must have seemed like an eternity. I love you. To my brothers and sister, I appreciate your advice, support, and guidance through the years.

As I move on, I realize that I may never pass this way again. I leave with a feeling of satisfaction that I believe I have offered a message of hope and not of despair. This has been an experience of a lifetime that I will never forget. I am forever indebted to each and every member of the team.

My words are dedicated to the memory of my father, Reverend John W. Dozier, and my mother, Viola E. Dozier. Dad was a Washington and Lee University law school graduate who decided the ministry was his calling. He was an avid and skilled writer. These words come from my mouth, but the underlying principles of honesty, decency, and caring come from both of your hearts. Dad, for all of those rejection letters you received over the years, you finally got published! And I believe you and Mom have spoken well.

Finally, thank you America for the First Amendment and free speech, without which this book would never have been written. We must be ever vigilant in protecting legitimate free speech on all flanks, but we must never forget that the greatest threat to our fundamental rights and values will come from the wolves in sheep's clothing.

ACKNOWLEDGMENTS FROM SUE SCHEFF

First and foremost, I have to thank my editor, Michele Matrisciani, for not only being one of the best editors in the world, but pushing me to limits I never thought I could reach. Her friendship and dedication brought this book from the seed of an idea to what you now hold in your hands. Having to open old wounds to tell my story made this a very difficult book to write, and without Michele, it simply would not have been done.

A special thanks to the team at Health Communications, Inc. (HCI), particularly Tom Sand, an early champion of the project, Carol Rosenberg, who spent endless hours working to get this book out on time, Kim Weiss, marketing master and tireless cheerleader, and Larissa Henoch and the art department who have proven yet again to be truly inspired.

Olivia, you have contributed your heart and soul to this book and have gone beyond your duties. You are a passionate, talented professional and a loyal friend. I am so grateful that our paths have crossed and look forward to collaborating with you in the future.

I must also acknowledge my friends and colleagues that stood by me even when it risked their own online reputations. Cyberstalkers are a malicious breed who are quick to go after innocent bystanders simply because of their association with the primary target of the stalkers' attacks. Those who were loyal to me put themselves in the line of sniper fire; in order to protect their privacy, I will not address these brave souls by name. But you know who you are and my gratitude to each of you is deep and everlasting.

There is another dear friend, Jeff Berryman, who survived an onslaught of cyberattacks but sadly lost his life last year. Jeff, the world isn't the same without you. You are truly missed.

I am deeply grateful to have been blessed with a wonderful family, and send them all my love for their unstinting support.

An *extra special thanks* to David Pollack, Michael Fertik, and the entire team at ReputationDefender, and my coauthor John Dozier Jr. These intelligent professionals have all fought to bring civilization to cyberspace and I am the lucky recipient of their wisdom, compassion, and guidance.

And finally:

To all of the people who have silently suffered and felt powerless while the very core of their lives has been violated by vicious keystrokes, and to the many individuals that have reached out to me for help or expressed appreciation for the hope my story has given them: I dedicate this book to you.

Foreword

Google™ is not God. Google is not the First Amendment, and it is not the truth. It is a machine. It may be the best machine invented in the past fifteen years, with myriad benefits for human knowledge and collaboration, but it is still just a machine that operates on rules devised by people. For that reason, it is both inherently fallible and subject to deliberate abuse.

It may be amazing that we actually have to *say* that Google isn't God or the equivalent of freedom of speech or informational gospel truth. But it is clear that many of us believe what shows up on the top of Google results is the most important, best, most accurate, most complete, most reliable, and most up-to-date information about the subject we are searching. From what is publicly understood about Google, it seems that the search engine scientists who work there try very hard to make the most democratically valued information rise to the top, on the basic operating theory that the wisdom of the crowd will, over time, tend to favor the best and most comprehensive websites that discuss a particular topic, be it animal, vegetable, or mineral, cabbages or kings.

But despite what may be Google's best efforts and intentions, the machine gets it wrong at least as often as it gets it right. The errors

and omissions of the world's search engines visit punishing consequences on the victims of erroneous, obsolete, incomplete, or false
information. Nonetheless, despite this mixed (and possibly worsen-
ing) track record, the rising primacy of Google as the world's most
important data channel seems to hoodwink many of us into believing what we see when it comes up on the top of Google search
results. The theory goes: if it shows up on Google, it must be true
and it's somehow the best information about the subject being
searched. It is clear that people make decisions based on what they
find in the top positions on Google: multiple visual "heat maps" published on the Internet have shown that the vast majority
of Google users look at the top few results and ignore everything
below them.

This is important for all of us, as we have become as searchable as
the subjects we crave information on. What shows up at the top of
Google can make or break our professional lives, our chances at
romance, and our ability to get into the school of our dreams. It is
far easier to harm someone and destroy their reputation on the
World Wide Web than it is to make that person look great or even
plain vanilla neutral. Blogs and discussion forums often enjoy more
prominence in search engines than newspapers and other edited professional journals. Under the rules of search engines as they exist
today, odd blog and forum corners of the Web can be turned into
powerful launch pads of interpersonal attack.

There are real-life consequences when someone aims to destroy
someone else on the Internet. It's all too easy to destroy another person on the Web. In cyber-slamming cases, victims are often intimidated into silence because they feel powerless and helpless, and their
first instinct is to shut themselves up so that things don't "get worse."

Sue, a victim herself, is a rare individual because she decided to stand up for herself on the Web, defend herself in the courts and online, and go about protecting herself and others in an assertive way. You may or may not agree with everything Sue and John have written, but we can all agree that the narrative they tell is an important one for the emerging discussion of Internet, speech, and the speech-shaping powers of Google.

Michael Fertik
CEO and Founder of ReputationDefender

All Rise

The day is September 19th, 2006, a Tuesday. It's a little before 2:30 in the afternoon and the weather is sunny, breezy, and beautiful in Fort Lauderdale, Florida. The surf is up just down the street and my stomach is riding a wild wave as the jury of six somberly files into the nearly empty courtroom.

I have no idea what to expect. My lawyer, David Pollack, leans a little closer and whispers, "Well, this is it. . . . " I wish there was something I could hold onto besides his words since my legs aren't feeling very steady as the bailiff, a very kindly looking older man, intones, "All rise."

This is a landmark case for Internet defamation, as no precedent has ever been set. My organization has been all but destroyed. My personal reputation dragged through such muck it makes a pig sty seem clean by comparison. David has prepared me as best he can for what the verdict might be. I'm already out over $100,000 with a second mortgage on my house to get this far, but if the jury finds in my favor and grants us even a tenth of that I'll feel vindicated.

The Honorable Judge John Luzzo, in flowing black robe and wearing his duties with appropriate dignity, takes his elevated seat on the bench and asks the foreman, "Has the jury reached a verdict?"

"We have, Your Honor." Perhaps in her midthirties, dark haired and pretty, she hands their verdict to the bailiff, who hands it to the judge—he nods in seeming approval—then back it goes from the judge to the bailiff to the foreman. The air is trapped in my lungs. I can't breathe. And then she begins to read, line by line, the jury's unanimous decision:

"For Parents' Universal Resource Experts . . ." (PURE, that's the organization I set up to help parents of troubled teens) ". . . we award $1,170,000 in compensatory damages as well as punitive damages of $2,000,000." Punitive, meaning to punish the defendant for what they've done, am I hearing this right? "And for Sue Scheff we award . . ."

Tears are streaming down my face while I watch David scribbling the numbers as the foreman keeps reading . . . and reading. David circles the final rough math and mutters in disbelief: "What? Over *ten million!*"

"Court is adjourned!" The loud thud of wood on wood as Judge Luzzo slams down his gavel reverberates in my ears. Nothing seems real. Even the jurors asking the judge for permission to personally speak with me, then approaching with open arms, seem like a waking dream. My unflappable attorney, so steady in court, is giddy as a kid with a mile-high cone of cotton candy on his first carousel ride once we're outside, fist punching the air and whooping, "I don't believe it! I don't believe it! This could be the biggest Internet defamation jury award in history!"

Being awarded a staggering amount of money for standing your ground when you've been deeply wronged is a wonderful thing. Having one's faith restored in the goodness of humanity after witnessing the underbelly of it is even more priceless.

I've been a victim of Internet defamation. I understand too well the sense of powerlessness, isolation, and unadulterated fear that if you tell someone your name and they decide to Google search you (it happens), you've suddenly gone from acquaintance to some *Fatal Attraction* monster who makes Hitler seem like a saint—a pariah to be avoided at all costs. It's a fate much worse than getting dissed by someone you thought was a friend only for another to clue you in on the latest mean gossip making the rounds. Internet defamation is another animal entirely—a cruel and vicious animal that often lacks a face and hides behind the computer screen in cowardly anonymity. Or so the "anonymous" think.

It is my sincere hope that by exposing my own ordeal, as well as the mistakes I made when trying to confront unfounded attacks on my character and business practices, that you might benefit from them both.

My name is Sue Scheff. This is my story.

❦

Unfortunately, there are too many Sue Scheffs out there. The victim of an online defamation attack can be a Fortune 500 company, a soccer coach, a Girl Scout leader, the singer in a boy band, your local dentist, a world famous plastic surgeon, a professional athlete, a college professor, that ex-lover, a government official, your minister, your spouse, or your children. I'm John W. Dozier Jr., founder of the Dozier Internet Law firm . . . and I fix problems. One such problem? Not content to sucker punch the elderly lady on a street corner and snatch her purse, miscreants have taken their activities indoors. Understandable, I guess. Winters can get a bit nippy and with global warming and all, summers are way too hot. So they now ply their trade on the Internet, carefully searching out "marks" in air-conditioned comfort while reclining in an overstuffed lounger swigging microbrews. But they aren't the only problems. The defamation predators of the web look like that friendly paper-boy, the church choir director, your child's best friend, or the guy or gal next door because, well, how should I say this … they are.

Sue has a great story to tell, but I have others to draw from as well. This is a very different kind of book, one that I hope you'll find both fascinating and enlighten-ing as Sue speaks from her personal experience and I offer my professional expert-ise. At the beginning of each chapter, you will meet Sue and read in her words the intricate and intimate details of her landmark $11.3 million court victory and the malicious deeds that led up to it. Following Sue's personal accounts, I will interject my sections (which are prompted by a change in typeface as has occurred here), and take you on a guided tour of the underworld of the web, show you the inside tricks of the trade, tell you how to know when you are a defamation target, walk you through the early warning signs, and train you on how to deal with the attack while maintaining your sanity and recovering your good name. From passive defense to high-powered offense, from rallying the troops to counterinsurgent maneuvers, you'll learn how to fight back and win. Of course, we'll cover what to do, and what not to do, when under attack. And you'll learn ready-made steps you can take immediately to turn back attacks on your name before they even start.

The cyberdefamation scourge sweeping the web today is destroying lives, careers, and businesses with no advance warning. The devastation is shock-ing and immediate. The risk is too high for you to ignore this new form of online personal terrorism. But you have to help yourself. There are no white knights and no one is going to come to your rescue. So take our stories, advice, and guidance as a wake-up call. You have the power to gain control of your good name and reputation before the nice boy who lives next door, who seems to always be sitting in his overstuffed recliner drinking a beer, decides to pay you and yours a little cybervisit. Strange things can happen on the web. Those under attack will at times feel out of touch with reality. Sue will tell you that she was no exception.

WE'RE NOT IN
KANSAS ANYMORE

I like to believe that John Donne was right when he said, "No man is an island, entire of itself," but when you've been swallowed up by the sense of isolation and helplessness that a mass attack on your character and reputation can bring, it sure can feel like you've been shipped to a leper colony, population of one.

I want to tell you about my life before a smoke monster known as cyberstalking, Internet defamation, whatever you want to call it, reared its ugly head and set out on a viral mission to squash me like a gnat.

Let's begin with my earlier book, *Wit's End: Advice and Resources for Saving Your Out-Of-Control Teen*, which tells my personal story about having an at-risk teenager—as so many parents do, there are so many out there—putting her in a program for teens who have become a danger to themselves and/or others, learning she was being abused in this program, then getting her back home in worse shape than when she left.

As a result of the trauma from our own experience, I established an organization to assist other families in similar circumstances, known as Parents' Universal Resource Experts (PURE). My goal wasn't to make mother lodes of cash to cruise the Caribbean in high season, but to acquire information and distribute it to families that needed help while facing their own parental nightmares. I'd been there. I understood. I wanted to do whatever I could to help. My motto was and is "learn from my mistakes, gain from my knowledge."

Since I have been painted by some others on the Internet as being a shrewd "con artist" who's always been in it for the money and loves nothing better than to dupe vulnerable families for my personal gain, let me go on the record (and it is on legal record) as saying nothing could be further from the truth. If someone needed help, no matter their circumstances, I would never, will never, turn them away. I have spent countless hours offering what assistance I can to distraught families without charge.

If you want to know more about that part of my story you can read all about it in *Wit's End*.

Although I wasn't exactly giving Warren Buffet a run for his portfolio, I have to say that for a while I truly had an embarrassment of riches. My work was incredibly rewarding; I had such a sense of purpose that I couldn't wait to get to my office bright and early, return a never ending list of calls, and reply to an avalanche of e-mails that would pile up faster than I could respond.

I especially enjoyed meeting the parents face to face. As great as the phone and computer are as a means of communication, there's nothing that can quite replace the human connection that's found in a look, a touch, a tear. There were a lot of those and they didn't just come from the parents who were desperate enough to seek me out. I can choke up right now remembering some of those conversations that took place in what seems like yesterday and yet was a lifetime ago. You don't forget those things; they become part of your emotional DNA.

The private meetings I had were more than offset by the amount of time I funneled into public relationships. My speaking engagements ranged from large conferences to small organizations: from the Kiwanis to local police stations; professional associations to PTOs; keynote speeches to luncheons. I would meet with adolescent therapists, juvenile probation officers, guidance counselors, the list goes on. My schedule was nonstop; it seemed as if I was constantly booked to talk about teen issues—trust me, there are a lot of troubled teens out there, it's a huge swath of our population, especially when you factor in the other family members who are affected.

There's something amazing about finding your passion. It's such a gift, meant to be shared, not hoarded or squandered. The innate joy we find in answering a true calling can't help but spill over into other areas of our lives. My own was so rich and vibrant that . . . I guess you could say that it made me shine inside and out, personally and professionally. And like a young mother fawning over a precious child, PURE was my baby. It was my beloved little gem that I'd raised on sacrifice and principle; that I built from the ground up, call by call, letter by letter, meeting by meeting.

Now the thing about being wrapped up in a cause, especially a worthy one, is that so much of your life is ruled by its needs. One of PURE's most intrinsic needs was a large Internet presence as a distribution system for offering up my guidance. That's how a significant number of families across America found us. An equally important need was the ability to maintain an unblemished reputation. We are, after all, talking about the welfare of children who are already at risk. And, if there was a third necessity of the highest order, it would be networking and creating an online community of trust by bringing together the right people, the right resources, and the right connections to solve the most pressing needs of our kids.

These three things—distribution, reputation, and community— were the brain, the spine, and the legs that enabled PURE and, by extension, myself to become regarded as one of the best go-to sources in the teen program industry. And like most industries, there's a certain octopus extension that flows in many directions and has a sweeping reach.

Due to the good reputation I had established within a very large network of contacts, I wasn't surprised to receive a phone call one day from an individual I'll refer to as M. Clark. It's a fictitious name. Although I don't believe in anonymous postings, my case has attracted an underbelly of Internet society that has wished me dead in graphic detail. For my own self-protection, and that of my children, I'll be using fictitious names where I deem them prudent, but nothing has been concealed with regard to the role these very real people have played in my life or the facts of my legal dealings with them.

Anyway, you'll be hearing a lot about M. Clark, and when she first contacted me, I didn't think to look her up online, just as it had never occurred to me to check myself out. Little did I know what a mistake that would turn out to be, and I was completely unsuspecting as Clark asked for some advice and assistance in having two sons removed from a teen program in Costa Rica that had received some bad press. I offered her my hand because she was distressed and I felt compassion for this woman whose ex-husband had placed their boys in the program.

While my child is the only child I have ever actually removed from a program's custody, a large part of my job is to educate parents who are often scared and trying to navigate blind through a strange and daunting industry labeled "teen help." I give them what guidance I can and, if appropriate, offer resources and information that may be of assistance. And, that's exactly what I did for M. Clark. I gave her some hopefully useful information, including the name of a consultant named Steve who might be able to assist her since he was familiar with the school and had recently been to Costa Rica. And that was it. I never billed her a dime; she never paid me a penny. Beyond the call she placed to me, for all I knew we'd never cross paths again.

If only that were the case.

Shortly after our conversation and prior to getting her sons back, Clark resurfaced on a now defunct private listserv called the IntrepidNet, sometimes referred to as Trekkers—a support group primarily for parents of troubled teens, many of whom were either in teen help programs or had previous experience with them.

The woman who started the listserv, a truly sweet and caring soul, died unexpectedly. Since we were good friends and I had accumulated so much knowledge about the subject everyone was dealing with, the listserv regulars looked to me to step into a surrogate position for her. I informally accepted the responsibility—after all, it wasn't a huge group, fluctuating in the range of 50 to 100 members who would come and go, post and lurk. This being a private list, invitations to new members needed to be approved. Judging from my brief interaction with Clark, she seemed well suited to the group and we had no reason to decline her request to join us.

So in she came.

At first all was as it should be. There was the usual give-and-take, being there for a listserv friend when they were feeling down or throwing cyberconfetti when things were looking up. We welcomed

Clark with open arms, offering her our collective support, well wishes, and prayers to get her sons back safely.

And she did. But then, something we had never encountered before began to happen.

After Clark got her sons back she contacted me privately, requesting access to a young woman who had been allegedly raped at the boys' facility. I had a friend who knew the girl's mother, and the friend asked if she was open to discussing the incident with other concerned parents. The mother said no, they just wanted their privacy. I relayed the outcome to Clark and, as far as I was concerned, there was nothing else to discuss. In addition to my empathy for the affected family, distributing private information is not only a good way to destroy a stellar reputation, it is ethically wrong, and that's a place I refuse to go.

Clark, however, took it upon herself to then go directly to the IntrepidNet/Trekkers listserv to get what she was after. What started as polite pleading became an insistent demand to score some immediate contact with this traumatized girl, via her mother or another liaison.

The listserv was stunned by Clark's badgering for what the member either didn't have to provide or wouldn't relinquish to her. Their common purpose had always been to protect the young, not expose, exploit, or intimidate them. Members approached me privately, expressing their distress and wanting to have Clark removed to restore some peace to the group.

I tried to mediate the issue with a post to the members that read, in part: "I am officially making this the end of the saga. If I can do this. We need to let this go on our listserv because it is going nowhere and taking up too much energy, and has also caused the loss of a valuable parent (in the sense that she is no longer on the list)."

Long story short: A valuable member had dropped out, Clark's hostility toward the listserv continued to ratchet up, and the webmaster expelled Clark from the list so she could no longer log in and cause havoc.

Why, you might wonder, was this woman so determined to make contact with a young victim that she would aggressively turn on a group of individuals who had supported her in her own time of need? None of us knew, which made the situation even more confusing and disturbing than if we'd at least had an inkling of Clark's motives. It would be over two years before witness testimony would shed some light on this mystery. Suffice it for now to say that, not surprisingly perhaps, money was involved.

More on that later.

After Clark was removed from the listserv and things got back on track there, I was going about business as usual, too. Meeting with parents, racing to keep up with speaking engagements and community service workshops, and covering all the other bases that seemed to be constantly loaded.

Of course a lot of those bases involved our website and the Internet. And, like most people, I used it for a lot more than an essential tool in my workbox. I still use Travelocity, MapQuest, and Weather. com on a regular basis. And it's hard to beat a search engine to check out local eateries, see what others are saying about movie reviews, or size up the countless other people, places, and things that might pique our curiosity or even have a potentially great impact on our lives.

But every now and then, the information we're counting on as being correct hits a glitch—like didn't MapQuest know that the off-ramp it said I should turn on is under construction and now I'm going to be a *lot* later than the five minutes I was already running behind to meet a friend for dinner at the new restaurant that got such rave online reviews?

Such is the entanglement of our day-to-day lives with the source of advice we've come to depend on for . . . just about everything, it seems. It's nothing less than amazing when you stop to think about what an intimate relationship we've forged with the "Information Highway" and just how broad an audience a single website can reach—especially open forums where virtually *anyone* can read what is being posted. As it turned out, while I was busy doing business and living life as usual, Clark was busy as well.

I received a heads-up from a parent on the IntrepidNet/Trekkers listserv, that Clark had found a new home at a public forum where she was venting her anger toward our members in general, and me in particular. I wasn't immediately too concerned. After all, I had actually tried to help Clark and it wasn't me who had gotten her kicked off our list—she had done that to herself by alienating her earliest supporters.

Still, I was curious about what she could be posting for anyone who cared to look, so I went online and did a Google search of my name for the first time in my life.

I hit the enter key and as my eyes moved down the first page of results I saw my name mentioned in some context I could not understand. It made no sense. I clicked on the result and I was *there*. Reading . . . and reading . . . and thinking, surely I couldn't be reading this right. Surely these words couldn't be about me, screaming out from the computer screen in stark black-and-white.

I sat back. Blinked a few times. Read it all again. I was too shocked to initially react beyond a blank stare. I believe I wrapped my hand around the necklace I was wearing just to be sure this was real and not some freak imagining. Then as the reality of what I was viewing began to slowly sink in, my thoughts crystallized into both a prayer and an expletive:

Oh. My. God.

Monsters of the Web

Scofflaw Personas

Someone's first vanity search on Google is all too often followed by the panic of seeing something unpleasant, and Sue wasn't facing just a little snark or criticism or statement of opinion. I'm not a psychiatrist, and I don't play one on TV, but I'd like to offer you some guidance as to who it is you need to protect yourself from on the web.

Today I'm a trial lawyer intent upon studying the body language and characteristics of jurors, witnesses, lawyers, and judges. I'm comfortable with reading people and images. But what is behind mere words is harder to figure out. How do you understand someone's personality, their tendencies, their idiosyncratic dispositions, their emotional stability, and even their motivation by simply studying words and sentences? Dealing daily with the "monsters of the web," you learn to identify the hot buttons, the angles, the finesse moves, and the brute force tactics that might just turn back an attack and make everything normal again. I'm a trial lawyer. Sometimes what I do is pretty. Sometimes the process is pretty ugly. That's just the way it is.

I've consulted with and worked for the city council member attacked in the midst of a race, the professional athlete fighting fake social network profiles, the high-profile reporter getting nailed by just about everyone, a lead singer battling a fake video, a "convicted child predator" who is anything but, the star high school quarterback attacked as he is being recruited, the actress constantly abused in forums by a jealous woman, the Silicon Valley entrepreneur who made enemies on the way up and is now the target of their rage, the Wall Street bigwig whose name is used in porn websites, the venture capitalist who can't raise money because of a relative's online rant, a high profile TV commentator fending off a "sucks" website, a lobbyist being dragged through the mud by opposing political operatives, and enough lawyers, doctors, realtors, and Indian chiefs to last a lifetime.

I've represented the honest CEO who was the subject of an online assassination discussion, complete with photos of his house and close-ups of his front porch. I've represented the business whose former employee gratuitously decided to send spam e-mail "on behalf" of his former employer to over 10 million people and ask for them to call its offices. I've helped the monastery and monks turn back attacks by a former parishioner, a Fortune 500 company that had a convicted sexual predator prominently and convincingly publicize his "appointment" to its board of directors, and I've helped moms protect their sons, dads protect their daughters, children protect their parents, and friends protect their friends.

Through all of these situations, and many more too numerous to list, I tend to always try and discern the motivation of the parties involved. That, of course, involves trying to figure out what kind of monster of the web lurks behind the smoke. There are often clues to the identity and persona of the source of an attack. Some really thorough research up front is needed to develop enough facts to make a good, educated guess. And over time as we have unmasked these attackers, one not only develops a sense as to the motivation, but, more importantly, an instinct as to what is coming next, which can lead to clues as to how the problem might be solved.

I've come up with short descriptions for the monsters of the web. They often employ anonymity by attacking from behind a virtual smoke screen. Envision them behind a curtain, pulling levers and emitting smoke and fire to disguise their humanity. They revel in their own corrupted belief of omnipotence and strike terror in the hearts of others. My job is to pull back the curtain, clear the smoke, end the wizardry, and send them back to Kansas on a balloon filled with their own hot air.

1. Pickpocket

This is the guy who used to wait on street corners for elderly ladies to pass. He enjoys attacking defenseless people and stealing covertly using deception. This type of blogger will steal your copyright-protected content, have the search engines push your prospective clients to his site, and then run ads and otherwise direct the traffic to your competitors. He could be an affiliate marketer for a competitor getting a share of the revenue, or he could simply be running Google or Yahoo ads on his site. Pickpockets also take great pleasure in stealing your trademarks . . . surreptitiously using your mark in hidden tags, meta tags, hidden redirect pages, or through a myriad of search engine optimization techniques you can easily learn more about by looking online, all in the hopes of redirecting your prospects to a competitor and taking money from you.

2. Wacko

We usually identify a wacko situation quickly. There are distinctive characteristics of his communications. The wacko is usually a "follower," someone looking to gain attention and recognition, but escalates what may have started as fair criticism into more and more outrageous claims. Most sophisticated business people immediately view the poster as a "nut case," particularly when an excessive amount of time or energy disproportionate to the merits of the subject is expended. But it is not easy for the typical browser on the web to see the pattern, usually spread over multiple web properties.

3. Druggie

Or, maybe "liquid courage" would be more appropriate. This guy is exactly what comes to mind. During the day this blogger is a normal guy, but at night he returns to the sanctity of his home, gets drunk or high, and goes out on the web looking for "hookups" and blogging on his "hang-ups." This guy is hard to detect as a fraudster, and sometimes won't recall the next day what he said online while under the influence. He posts aggressive, false, and arbitrary attacks on whatever issue of the day (or night) catches his fancy.

4. Alien

No, not from another world. But from overseas. In a far, far away place, without any treaty with the United States, in a country without an effective legal system and no notion of business or personal property ownership rights. Many of these types operate out of certain Russian provinces, but the blogs, postings, and communications appear to be from the customer down the street. This individual usually has an ulterior motive, often working with the criminal discussed below. He has no fear, until he takes a vacation to Turkey and U.S. federal agents grab him for extradition, which is exactly what happened on a case in the not-so-distant past.

5. Nerd

This is the guy who is scared to talk with a girl, but behind the keyboard, all alone, morphs into a Casanova. This empowerment of anonymity creates an omnipotent persona, and for the first time the nerd feels the effect of power and control, gets an adrenaline buzz when he exercises it, and he exercises it often, usually creating or perpetuating a volatile situation in which he feels he can outsmart the "opposition." There is no principle involved. His blog postings are all about the adrenaline. It is hard to know if you are dealing with this type online . . . his posts are intelligent and on their face credible. But, once you identify the nerd blogger, he cowers and goes away, usually forever.

6. Rookie

Enjoy debating a thirteen-year-old? They are out on the net acting like adults, posting statements, and playacting like a grown-up. The challenge, of course, is that most people reading the posts have no idea these are coming from a kid.

The tip-off can be the utter immaturity of the posts, but most often the kids can sound credible criticizing, for instance, a CPA's method of calculating ROI for REIT holdings, because they can mimic earlier posts. There is no insidious motive here; just kids having fun as the hormones kick in. But the readers of the blog posting don't know that.

7. Sadist

This person attacks others, causes pain, and revels in the results in ways not worthy of mention. He loves to create, direct, control, and unleash a firestorm of criticism about you or your company just to create pain and damage. This type of person may often be the prime instigator of the online attacks, and tightens the noose by escalating the attack rapidly, almost as if in an obsessive state. You will find a sadist going to many sites and blogging, and he usually lets you know it was him because he uses his real moniker. He has characteristics of a stalker, and he is most likely to be the one that starts recommending direct physical violence against individuals. This person is not motivated by money, but by the pure enjoyment of pain being visited upon innocent parties.

8. Bankrupt

No, not morally bankrupt. Actually bankrupt . . . no money, no assets, no prospects for work, and nothing to lose. This blogger posts without fear of the consequences or any regard for the truth because "you can't get blood out of a turnip," "you can't get water from a rock," and all those other sayings handed down, I surmise, through generations of his family. This is usually not a smart guy, but his postings are damaging and inflammatory. Many will own and control blogs without any concern about the consequences of liabilities that might arise through the perpetuation and "enhancement" of posts, and sometimes will post to their own blog and act like it was from a third party.

9. Criminal

Career criminals, no less. Like the convicted felon running a sophisticated extortion scheme against a very prominent business. Or the owner of an open blog avoiding service of process with guard dogs protecting his compound. The thieves and crooks of the world are online today, and the criminals often have both an organization and a highly effective and surprisingly coordinated operational plan in place to target a business. Rumors of $500,000-a-year payoffs seem to promote this problem, which emanates from more of a "mobosphere" (the mob effect arising from a blogger attack) than the blogosphere.

10. Mis-Leader

This person is in no manner a leader. This blogger has a hidden agenda, but he just makes it sound like he is a totally objective commentator. He can create an appearance of authority and the casual visitor to his blog does not question the legitimacy. This type of persona is hard to figure out. One of the most pervasive practices is to control a blog and allow negative posts against all except his generous advertisers. Another common technique involves omission: not disclosing conflicts of interest or the existence of a business or personal relationship because the readers of the blog will totally discount the commentator's posts as unreliable and biased.

These are the types of characters who are serious risks to you and yours. You'll hear about some of their exploits from Sue and about others from me. For now, just know that there are dangerous strangers in your online neighborhood.

Don't get me wrong about this book. While you get a good sense of the characters out there, we are addressing unlawful and illegal conduct. We aren't focused on "semi-libel" or some snark problem. We aren't offering guidance on how to manage public relations when faced with a legitimate disgruntled customer's comments. And we aren't offering spin-control guidance.

We are addressing the damage that can be caused by bad conduct. We're focused on that .0001 percent of the online world that hides behind complexities (technical, societal, and legal) to attack the very fabric of our society by redefining truth via mob opinion. My thoughts focus on the tainting of truth through illegal or unlawful means. Attacks that threaten your reputation, your good name, and your right to enjoy life and protect your family and livelihood from miscreants and scofflaws. The good news is that a lot of our advice is proactive in nature; guidance you can start using today to build up defenses in case you become a victim.

Free speech today allows one to ignore civility and spout profane, uncouth, rude, and outrageous comments online within certain parameters. But the line between protected online speech and yelling "fire" in a virtual theatre is yet to be fleshed out. In a more concrete sense, free-speechers argue that labeling a competing business a "scam" is an opinion, not defamatory, and therefore protected free speech. On the other hand, I believe it very much depends upon the context of the speech. But this book is not a one-sided debate about the nuances of free speech, fair use, privacy laws, the First Amendment, and defamation. I'll leave debates like whether it is proper to publish photos of underage child abuse victims as they leave the courthouse to others for now. On the other hand, I'd be pleased to discuss the mob waiting outside a virtual courthouse ready to take the law into its own hands and conduct a very public offline and online lynching of a wrongfully-charged defendant.

We write all about the scofflaws of the web, those that act unlawfully, those who often support the tools they use, and what can be done to stop them. Scofflaws are the characters that not only violate laws, but do so with contempt. You've probably seen the type on those cable TV police shows . . . fighting the police and claiming discrimination and brutality and innocence as crack pipes are falling from their britches. The legality of their misconduct would only be debatable in the minds of the most jaded free-speech expansionists and privacy fanatics.

I don't understand lawyers who appear as talking heads on TV and decry the lack of laws governing online misconduct. They should be using their voices to inform you about the laws we do have, and what they mean. It strikes me that it is actually worse to ignore laws already in place than to suggest that no such laws exist. The web is the Wild West. But anyone who would suggest that no laws existed when the forces of law and order faced off with open banditry at the O.K. Corral in Tombstone, Arizona, would be wrong. Are our laws problematic, ambiguous, ill-advised, shortsighted, incomplete, outdated, and symptomatic of a level of inexactness and misunderstanding? Yes. But Congress and state legislatures and judges have not outright ignored the legal issues confronting our society. They just haven't got them right yet. Lawyers, judges, and legislators need to do a better job embracing the laws as they exist today rather than being intimidated by the subject matter and denying their existence. And each of you can play a mighty role in forcing real reform and change through the legislative process. We'll be discussing needed changes and how you can make a difference in the pages to come.

We hope to empower everyone to understand the risks, develop a healthy appetite for caution, and address the oncoming fears head-on. So, what exactly is there to fear? The loss of your good name and reputation, to start. But that's just for starters. Sue describes the online world as an "octopus that flows in many directions and has a sweeping reach." I agree. And it is called Google.

The tentacles of a web presence are inextricably managed, and indeed controlled, by this mighty online commerce platform best known for its search engine. Today, everyone seems to be using Google searches to replace the old way of checking up on people and businesses. Gone are the days of personal references and credit reports. Today, the real valuable stuff, at least for inquiring minds, is in the bowels of the online world, and a search is seemingly unbiased, revealing the good with the bad. You'll hear more about the inherent bias in Google's search engine results later. For now, understand that attacks focus on adding bad results, and getting rid of good results, when someone searches for you on Google.

In fact, the monsters of the web owe their existence to Google. They measure their worth to society by the Google page rank (a relative measurement used by Google to indicate the importance of a page in its eyes) of their latest attacks, tracking search results like a college football poll. There must be a real sense of power in being able to decide who you will ruin today as you arise each morning. Skip the caffeine and go straight to the jugular. And the monsters of the web are thieves in the worst way. They steal your name and your reputation, strip from your grasp the opportunities our America offers, convert your pride to embarrassment and your honor to shame. The sword they wield is Google, playing the role of the powerful aircraft, laden with misery soon to come and without rival as a delivery mechanism. And the major package to be delivered is the Google Bomb.

When the Road Forks, Take It

Google Bomb

Why is Google so important? Because everyone is coming to the Google party. If you want to visit, you don't need directions to Mountain View, California. You don't need directions from the San Francisco airport. I bet you could go up to a good ole country boy on some back road in Georgia, listen intently to his directions to take the fork in the road when you get to it, and still easily find Google with no further assistance. Searching online is becoming synonymous with Google. "Googling" is becoming a coined verb for searching online, much to Google's consternation. But have you ever stopped to consider who is really searching for you?

That prospective employer.
And your boss.
The bank.
Your child's teacher.

Your social club.

The kids' colleges of choice.

Your credit card company.

The local public utility.

Cable television.

Your trash collector.

The Little League.

Boy Scouts, Girl Scouts, and just about every charitable or nonprofit to
   which you offer your time.

The parents of your children's friends.

Your children's friends.

Your children.

Your children's children.

And so on for generations to come.

Your tennis partner.

Your workout companion.

The neighbor next door.

Next weekend's date.

Your classmates.

And anyone and everyone you know.

Your competitors in business.

Your clients or customers.

The vendors.

Job candidates.

The Press.

And just about everyone who does business with you.

The monsters of the web know all about how important the Internet is to you. And they know the buttons to push. If you are a stay-at-home mom, they'll scare you with suggestions of home invasion. If you are a lawyer, they attack your intellect. A plastic surgeon becomes a "butcher." Ministers are sexual deviants. The athlete is on steroids. The debutante is anorexic. The builder uses rotten lumber. The police are drunks. And on and on. They cut to the core. No doubt that security for moms, intelligence for lawyers, manual dexterity for surgeons, fidelity for ministers, natural ability for athletes, health for beauty queens, structural integrity for home builders, and sobriety for cops are core issues. And those are the targets of the monsters of the web. Picture this in your mind:

One day a not-so-friendly acquaintance spitefully decides that you should be labeled a "deadbeat parent" for owing child-support arrears of over $100,000. It's published on a newspaper forum by a jealous coworker, a competitor, or a local bully . . . it does not matter. "Someone" sees it and comments on a community website that the local newspaper has you listed as a deadbeat parent. And off it goes, within days taking over the first five pages of results on Google. Years from now some of the comments and posts will remain, indexed for all to see when your name is searched. Unless your name is Tiger Woods or Barack Obama, recently voted the two most recognized faces on the planet, in which case the results may fortunately be buried for posterity's sake due to the massive coverage taking up the first couple of hundred Google results.

The problem is, of course, that you have never missed a child-support payment in your life. In fact, you and your wife still live happily at home with all of your kids. You start calling a dozen or so of your old girlfriends from what seems like a century ago and inquire as to how they are doing, how their kids are, and not so subtly asking each if there is anything you should know. Assured no skeletons are lingering in the closet, you go visit the commentary

on the websites that dominate your online reputation. New posts are now coming at a rapid rate about your telephone calls . . . you are reportedly on the
prowl, calling women and propositioning them. And the comments all include
links with your name to the other lies.

Finally, you can take no more. You go online, and since you don't want to be
obvious, you act as if you are someone else, and start defending yourself. This
feeds the flames, posts accuse you of using an alias, and you run off as quickly
as possible. As you end the web browser session with a crisp click, you skip
closing down the programs and go straight to powering down your laptop.
Then you go and remove the power cord from your computer, remove the
Internet connection cord, and go over and unplug your router. You pull the
car into the garage, turn off the outdoor floodlights on the house, lock all the
doors, pull the drapes and shades, turn down the volume on the TV, and you
wait. I have no idea what you are waiting for, but you've just gone through a virtual mugging and, frankly, you're not handling it well.

And for the next two years, credit applications are denied, your cable television company insists upon prepayment, that Little League head coaching
position goes to a pal of yours, the kids don't have as many "sleepovers," clients
of your business ask a lot more questions, and party invitations evaporate.

You've been Google Bombed. And as you seek cover and look for a fallout
shelter, the best directions offered are that "you can't get there from here."

It's true that all roads at one point led to Rome. Now they lead to Google, no
matter what fork you take.

I field calls from all over the world on what seems like a daily basis. A long
description of a particularly vicious attack is usually followed by a simple
question from me: "Do you realize it could get much worse?" As I list three or
four more things that could happen I hear nothing but a stunned silence, a
choice expletive, and a whispered prayer. Yes, it can get much, much worse.
And for Sue, it did.

NO GOOD DEED SHALL GO UNPUNISHED

"Sue Scheff is destroying lives . . . I want others to know. If you don't want to hear it then go elsewhere. You support her . . . I am posting on this board to tell others about PURE, Inc., and all the players who are associated with PURE, Inc."

Even years later these words have the impact of a sucker punch I didn't see coming. It's one of many posts on the open forum where most of the damage was done and later presented as exhibits to the Florida jury that set a historic precedent with their stunning award for PURE—and me—on that beautiful September day in 2006. But I'm getting ahead of myself. Turning back the clock to August of 2003, when the above post exploded from my computer screen, my initial shock subsided enough for a good dose of anxiety to kick in. *How many other posts had appeared on this forum, saying such terrible things about me? Was it just Clark? Or were there other people bad-mouthing me, and what on earth could I have done to deserve such a thing?*

PURE had really taken off at the time, and I was thrilled to not only provide assistance to those in need, but to be able to make a living—not a tremendous amount of money, but certainly enough to get by—with the priceless benefit of doing something I love. There aren't many people who can say that and I was counting my blessings. In between researching and evaluating programs and offering guidance and support to the hundreds of parents looking for help, my days were full.

I want to stress that I decided long ago that I would never charge parents for my time or services, so my sustenance depended, and still does, upon fees from various programs that meet with my personal approval. Not that my recommendations have ever been contingent on receiving a fee. There have always been programs deserving of recommendation that never compensated me for sending families their way. I go into such details on my website, www.helpyourteens. com/faq.php, if you'd like to know more.

Anyway, as soon as I got past the initial shock of learning that I, Sue Scheff, was destroying lives, it became apparent that I wasn't the only one getting bashed. A post from the day before involved someone from the IntrepidNet/Trekkers listserv, who had questioned Clark about a statement she'd made concerning me and Steve, the individual whose name I had passed along when Clark had first contacted me, asking for help in retrieving her sons from a teen program in Costa Rica.

"Steve stayed and visited another school while in Costa Rica at my expense", *Clark responded to the inquiry.* "He lied. I have the bills, the cancelled receipts, and the proof that Steve took me for a ride. I have the emails from Sue and her pushing me to take Steve with me. I have it all!!! You better learn to be right about what you say . . . You know nothing about what has happened. Keep your mouth shut until you do! Nobody knows the extent of what my boys and I have been through, you idiot. Why do you continue to be so stupid? One more thing. You said, 'I'm not clear on some of this.' Are you clear on ANYTHING?"

And then, following the thread, I read this, another response from Clark to someone else who was wondering what all the fuss was about:

"Sue Scheff, she recommended Steve, the consultant. He stirred it up good. He was the biggest con of all. Just like Sue. He took us for a ride. A money ride. She is responsible for her part in that."

Well, I guess that explains where some of Clark's anger was coming from. Only, I never pushed her to take anyone with her to the school. I simply gave her the name of the one person I knew within the industry who was familiar with that particular program *and* Costa Rica, where I had never been. I had nothing to do with Clark's decision to hire him, no knowledge of the financial details they worked out for him to accompany her. Steve was an educational consultant who seemed to have the credentials she was looking for, and if indeed he took financial advantage of Clark, that's very wrong, but I had no part in it and most definitely was not a recipient of any ill-gotten gain.

Needless to say, at this point my stomach had hit the floor faster than my jaw could follow. I'm trying to find the words to express the initial effect this had on me physically, mentally, emotionally, and . . . there's just no way to adequately describe the indescribable. And, even if there were, how could I possibly describe what I felt when things quickly got worse? Or, as John has said, much, much worse.

Once I found this open forum where my name and PURE had become a hot topic, I watched in stunned disbelief as Clark kept posting, faster and faster, in what seemed to be an escalation to some point of no return. Within a few days, she posted:

"Sue, you are going down. I bet you are scared to death! You know you are going down . . . because what you have done and are doing is wrong!!!!"

If you would, just for a moment, try to put yourself in my shoes. What would you do? Would you respond? Would you reach out and attempt to reason with someone who was so certain of their resentment against you, even if you didn't understand it yourself? Would you stay silent and hope the waking nightmare would just go away?

Only you can decide what you might have done in the same circumstance (and John can tell you what you *should* do), but being the one in the thick of it, I made the best decision I could at the time: I did not immediately react. I kept my silence. I did have friends, however, on the Trekkers listserv who did not keep theirs. Without my knowledge they took it upon themselves to contact Clark via e-mail and even phone, asking her to stop what was rapidly escalating into a full-blown attack—which only got worse with each well-intended attempt at intervention.

I believe in accountability, and in all honesty some of my supporters got caught up in the heat of the moment and said some things to Clark that were better left unsaid. But it also became clear that no matter how diplomatically, reasonably, or intelligently my defenders tried to intervene, their attempts to mediate only fueled the fire that was accelerating at a breakneck pace.

Did I say a fire? Make that more like a tsunami on speed.

One of the early waves of punishment I didn't see coming were publicly posted e-mails marked "Confidential" that had been privately exchanged between me and Clark in, shall we say, happier days when

I was trying to provide some good-faith assistance. Not that anyone reading the open forum would gather as much after a neat bit of editorial commentary to cast me in the worst possible light. Others were not immune to the same public exposure that had been intended for Clark's eyes only.

Why was I being targeted? Why me? Why the backlash against anyone who dared to defend me? These questions kept rolling through my head, and while I didn't have any answers, it did begin to dawn on me that I could be experiencing an unexpected repercussion directly related to the sort of business I was in.

Although virtually anyone can become a target for cyberattacks, I started to realize that certain industries and the individuals associated with them might run a higher risk than others, due to the sort of traffic and personalities they have a tendency to attract. In the field of at-risk teens and the various programs that address the troubling issues they and their families are facing, a lot of strong emotions can surface: fear, anger, confusion, vulnerability, resentment, and deep love. When a teen is placed in a good program that results in the desired outcome for them and their families, it's a beautiful thing that alters the course of lives in a wonderful, positive way.

However, not all endings are happy ones, and bad programs have done terrible damage to the young in need of help, often leaving emotional scars that even time may never heal. Again, I've talked at length about this industry and my personal experience with it in *Wit's End*. That book is about a very different subject than what this one is all about, but there is little doubt my involvement in a particularly sensitive area of social services had a lot to do with my exposure for retaliation, no matter how undeserved it might be.

Thinking back, let's consider who would have been taking a look at, or actively participating in, the open forum where all this damage was being done to my good name and the reputation of my organization. The primary emphasis was on troubled teen programs. Parents looking for advice and resources could find the link with the key words typed into a search engine. Professionals such as school counselors, family therapists, or psychologists would be good candidates while doing a little online research. And then there are those who have been burned and want to vent, who adopt assumed identities, such as "Dysfunction Junction" (one of my more vocal detractors), or anonymously want the world to know their opinion (lots of those), or proudly sign their names as they post and post and post—which is exactly what Clark had no qualms about doing. In fact, the handy little post tracker beside her name indicates that she had 556 posts between January 18, 2003, and July 24 the same year.

Five hundred and fifty-six posts in six months. Wow. And that's before I even found out about the website!

On the heels of all my stunning new discoveries, another development suddenly surfaced. Just as I had protectors unsuccessfully trying to come to my aid, Clark found an ally who was far more successful in promoting the ongoing attacks: the founder of the website from which the attack campaign originated.

What made this person such a willing recruit? Apparently one of her purposes in founding the forum was to provide a website for those with bad program experiences to report. And, as you might guess, she was able to commiserate after having had a damaging experience herself.

There are three main characters in this story whose names I have changed for reasons already explained, and L. Smith, Clark's second-in-command, is number two.

I would be interested in what personality types John thinks Clark and Smith fall into when it comes to the monsters of the web he was earlier discussing. "Mobosphere" is a term he coined, and I can tell you that a mob mentality did begin to take over, led in part by Smith who zealously took up the charge and protected Clark while bashing me with equal amounts of fervor.

For example, when one of my own defenders piped up on the forum with a post that reads in part, "[Clark], you have made accusations that you cannot back up because that's exactly what they are, accusations, not the TRUTH!" It was Smith who replied, "Divide and conquore (sic) isn't going to work here, you sad, angry little people."

The "accusations" of course, consisted of the malicious statements that were gathering momentum on Smith's website in the form of open posts, most of them initially authored by this gang of two.

And as I watched this whole crazy thing escalate faster than a speeding bullet and become more powerful than a locomotive, I started to notice something else happening. Something just as scary and equally out of my control: when I did a Google search on Sue Scheff and PURE, the open forum where my organization and I were being trashed had begun to inch up, closer and closer to the top results.

The Three Amigos: SEO

Search Engine Optimization

A little insight into how people search on the web is helpful because that is at the center of many online attacks. Understanding the three amigos, the three indispensable components involved in gathering, organizing, and presenting information online, is essential. The first is the search function (S), the second is the engine driving results (E), and the third is optimization

(O) for the purpose of influencing the results of a search.

So if a tree falls in the woods, and no one hears or sees it, did it fall? Yeah, it did. But who cares? Only the guy who had the misfortune to park his ATV under it and go off on a hike, I guess. If someone online publishes hurtful, private, and false information about you on the web, and no one finds it, who cares? You might, but it is usually not a huge deal. It can become a big deal, though, thanks to search engines. And that's what Sue was about to find out as she watched the forum comments reach to the top of the search results when someone searched her name on Google.

I've heard more than one person tell a new acquaintance to "just Google me." You won't hear that phrase in this book because we respect Google's trademark protection efforts to keep its name from becoming a verb. Google, as I am sure you know, is primarily a search engine website running electronic programs ("spiders") all over the Internet so it can capture the results and index them. Algorithms are used to figure out what should be presented when a search is conducted. If you own a restaurant, and your competition seems to always be ahead of you in search results when someone searches for a restaurant in your area of town, Google thinks they are more important than you. Maybe they are using legitimate means to get where they are, or maybe the dishwasher, in between seatings, is going online and raving about how great their food is. Clearly he has dirty hands in more ways than one. That's a problem for you, but probably not the problem that you really need to be most worried about.

You should understand that getting a top result on a search could be very profitable for a business. I'm sure the first result returned, which would be a link to a website, for a search like "refinance my mortgage" made someone very rich. Even first page results, which on a Google results page is the top ten, can be highly sought after and profitable positions. Consequently, when Google began taking off in popularity (now by far the search engine of choice in the United States), businesses and consultants ran over to the U.S. Patent Office, found the Google patent for how the algorithms work, and tried to build websites catering to the key indicators of popularity and relevance. This is called "SEO" (search engine optimization), and it means what it says . . . optimizing the characteristics of a website for high search engine results.

There is "on page" SEO, which includes things you can do on your own web-page or web property to be indexed high, and there is "off page" SEO, which involves actions you can take elsewhere on the web, like building up links, registering with directories, and creating a buzz about yourself. Those are important terms because, ultimately, the entire goal of prevalent search engines today is to return the most reliable and relevant indexed results. The better the results, the more people will be happy using the search engine. That means more eyeballs to notice, and fingers to click on, those little "sponsored ads" that you see on the results page. Every click makes the search engine money. So the search engine ranks what it finds based upon the authority of the result, and a heavily linked site or post is seen by a search engine as the online world's vote that the site is authoritative. I'll spend some time later discussing how this is unscrupulously used to attack a target.

My explanation so far is simplistic. Suffice it to say that an entire industry now exists on the web that focuses solely on trying to get top ranking for web results to drive traffic and increase sales for businesses. Also, there is another form of SEO that has taken off over the past couple of years: social network SEO. As you might imagine, this has everything to do with using social networks to rank higher.

You will need to understand SEO, at least at a high level, to appreciate what others with bad intent can do to you. And fortunately what you can do for yourself. So imagine these "SEO" techniques, instead of being used positively to build up an "online reputation" (which is a key phrase to understand and basically refers to the online image of a person or business based upon search engine results), are used to attack. You wonder why the place next door is booming with business all of a sudden—they even had lines out the door and people with children waiting in the cold rain without umbrellas!—while your restaurant sat empty . . . except for the people at the bar waiting for their reservation to be called next door. Well, Mr. Dishwasher decided to start dissing your restaurant with lies . . . roaches on the walls, glass in the ice bins, food poisoning galore. And because he read this book, he knows exactly how to SEO those posts so the defamatory comments are showing up in search results when someone checks out your reputation. Okay, let's be realistic. He probably didn't read the book. Someone read it to him.

How big is this problem? An entire industry appropriately called "reputation management" has arisen to deal with it. These consultants (yes, I'll tell you some of their secrets later) are hired by people and businesses alike to either build an online "firewall" against a defamation attack or deal with repelling an attack and rehabilitating a reputation. There are ways to push down the negative Google results and move positive search results ahead. Sound familiar? Yep, SEO is being used to counteract SEO.

So as Sue is attacked in the early stages, these outrageous attacks are prominent for all to see when she is searched. Businesses spend great sums each year making sure this does not happen to them. But how do individuals, families, or small businesses protect themselves? There's no online marketing budget to tap into. The good news is that there is a lot you can do at no cost and with relatively little effort.

Neither Sue nor I are against the First Amendment to the U.S. Constitution or the concept of free speech. We're not writing about snarking or sarcasm or parodies or fair use. We aren't focused on helping businesses with public relations and improving their customer satisfaction levels. This book is about the perpetration of vicious and unlawful attacks using falsehoods and pretense to ruin people's lives.

Sue is just beginning to understand she has a problem. A big problem. Growing bigger by the day. No "three amigo salute" is going to save the day, to be sure.

A Sweater with a Target on the Back

The Initial Response

The biggest challenge you will face when confronted with an attack on your good name is resolving a confounding problem. Let's assume that you are not intimately familiar with the three amigos: search, engine, and optimization (SEO). Do you sit back and take it? Do you strike out against your attackers, knowing in your heart and mind that while you will feel a sense of satisfaction the action might very well lead to more severe responses from your foes? The helpless feeling of being torn between your heart, your mind, and your soul on the one hand, and good judgment on the other, has been part of society ever since Eve felt her first hunger pains. There's the rub.

> To be or not to be, that is the question;
> Whether 'tis nobler in the mind to suffer
> The slings and arrows of outrageous fortune,
> Or to take arms against a sea of troubles,
> And by opposing, end them. To die, to sleep;
> No more; and by a sleep to say we end
> The heart-ache and the thousand natural shocks
> That flesh is heir to — 'tis a consummation
> Devoutly to be wish'd. To die, to sleep;
> To sleep, perchance to dream. Ay, there's the rub . . .

Hamlet's soliloquy has inspired many a commentator to try and divine the true meaning of the words. Many read the choice between the life of action ("to be") and the life of silent acceptance ("not to be") as Hamlet's primary focus.

In this respect, what you do about the online arrows of your misfortune is a big decision. It's a bit of an overstatement in most instances to suggest that by taking arms against attacks you will be committing online suicide. But sometimes it is true. If you think that offering up a defense will lead to absolution by your foes, or contrition by your enemies, then you are likely very, very wrong. The more you object, and the more you take up arms directly against your "sea of troubles," the more problems will likely arise. Look at Sue's situation. Didn't it escalate as her friends jumped in to defend her? So let's talk about that sea of troubles and see if Hamlet was onto something.

You are the lucky homeowner of a beautiful summer home on an East Coast barrier island. Every summer your wonderful view of the mighty Atlantic gets better. The sand dune that used to be an annoyance because it blocked your view of the dolphins frolicking in the waves grows shorter. And every summer the path to the beach, through that deep, hot sand, up and over the dune, gets easier to navigate even with the growing collection of plastic toys, beach chairs, coolers, sports equipment, and other absolutely essential accessories you haul. Life is good.

But one morning you wake up to the sound of a bulldozer next door. Your neighbor has decided to make life really, really good. He is leveling the sand dune on his property and will in short order be enjoying a wonderful view and easy ocean access.

You first notice the dark lines on your neighbor's newly minted beach volleyball court located, conveniently, where the old dune used to reside. As the full moon approaches, the water line reappears each morning closer and closer to his house. You know it's a high-tide mark, and a sign of trouble to come. Your neighbor, however, appreciates that his volleyball court base is being compacted to an almost perfect consistency by this welcome natural benefactor.

Over time, the crowds seem to grow along the beach, although the tourist bureau is reporting a drop in tourists. Little do you know it's because the waterline is moving closer to your treasured vacation retreat, pushing beach-goers up against the dune line out of necessity. And then, as you read the head-lines of the morning paper, your visions of a good life at the ocean are turning into a personal "sea of troubles."

You see, the city council has just released a report that predicts the entire first row of beachfront homes will be underwater in three years. You are on a barrier island, a mere spit of land intended by nature to migrate toward the mainland. Septic systems are already failing, the remaining dunes will soon be gone, the beach will disappear. Immediate actions are mandated: special taxes enacted to build seawalls, sea grass planted, sand fences installed, mas-sive sand-replenishment programs undertaken, and homes with failing sep-tic systems condemned. How are things now? Your path to the beach is obstructed, and an orange "condemned" sign is firmly affixed to your neigh-bor's front deck with little BB holes in it from the kids down the block using it as a target. And you wonder how long you have.

Do you just abandon your dream house? Or do you fight back? And if you fight back, is all for naught? By building that personal seawall, or by installing the jetty, will these seemingly prudent acts be suicidal? Is the entire island a lost cause, a soon-to-be relic of the past that one day will be discovered by underwater explorers who could not have imagined anyone foolish enough to build on what was once a barrier island?

There's the rub. How do you know what to do when under an attack? Do you sit back and suffer the misfortune of being the target? Or do you take up arms? And by responding, do you give your attackers a neatly wrapped present of slings and arrows? Consider the likely gift from them in return: an orange sweater with a target on the back!

The first and most important step in managing an online attack is to figure out whether it can be ignored. Ask yourself these questions in the evaluation stage:

1. No matter what was said, is it likely to be seen?
2. If it is seen, is it perceived as credible by those who matter to you?
3. If it sounds credible, is it damaging, now or in the future, to you or yours?
4. If damaging, could it be the start of a bigger attack?

Is it likely to be Seen?

Where is it showing up in Google results when your name is searched? This is the biggest issue. If it is not present on Google search results, then there is often no need to worry. But if it is, monitor it daily and see the direction it is moving. Momentum is important because a defamatory post buried in the depths of Google's results today could be the number one result when you are searched tomorrow. To take this a step farther, you can begin to get a sense of the broader picture. Is the post "SEO'd" to intentionally and effectively target you? You may not be able to figure this out, but a professional can often decipher intent by simply viewing and researching the attack page and related or participating online properties. If you can figure out the motivation, you can begin to understand the post in proper context and map out a much more effective response.

Is it credible?

Is the posting anonymous? Or has someone actually used his real name, which lends credence to the comment. Does it sound legitimate? Details imply truth. Is it "over the top" and an amalgamation of disjointed allegations joined with poor grammar and vulgarity that places the source in a poor light? Are others "piling on" in agreement?

Is it damaging?

One of the most difficult things to do is to ignore an outright lie told about you. But in the online world, it needs to be done. The most egregious forms of attack target your ethics and morals, particularly in relation to family and business. You may not like that someone is criticizing your appearance or making fun of you online. It's often tasteless and inappropriate. But if someone claims you are a horrible soccer player, or certain body parts are not real, or you are a loser, set aside your pride and ask yourself if it really is hurting you, your family, your profession, or your business. Use discretion. Don't sweat the small stuff. You'll go crazy. I recommend you have a friend take a look and tell you whether the content is a problem. When under attack, the victim often either overreacts or ignores the issue. You are looking for a balanced, objective perspective on the damage the attack may visit upon you, your family, your business, your reputation, and your life.

Could it be the start of bad things to come?

In and of itself, is the post a sign of bad things to come? Nipping a problem in the bud is important. As a business, a seemingly hurtful comment from a legitimate customer could be dealt with in an open and conciliatory manner and defuse any potential onslaught to come. But, honest complaints are unfortunately not what we are addressing. Is the false comment located on a site that has a history of "followers" vociferously engaging in new issues? As an extreme example, if a single comment makes it onto Slashdot.com, a website focused on tech news for techies, the comments all over the web and resulting website traffic can be overwhelming in a matter of hours ("slashdotted"). And importantly, are there threats in the post about what is to come next? If you'll recall in Sue's case, she was warned: Sue you are going down, along with some other choice words of warning. That's a red flag.

Make sure you approach the problem and possible solutions realistically. No one is going to be able to force Google to pull down results pointing to false and defamatory commentary absent a court order or request by the website owner. And getting an injunction is an expensive process with many complicating factors. If you think the site is going to readily pull down the content, the vast majority of the time the site will refuse to do so. In fact, there is every reason for them not to change content, including self-preservation under Section 230 of the Communications Decency Act (CDA), which is the federal law that grants immunity to website owners for defamation posted by third parties. All the owner has to do is refuse to edit or remove anything and the immunity applies without exception. Which, in turn, means that you can rarely convince a website to get rid of outrageous lies and attacks. Section 230 of the CDA should be the "Online Toxic Waste Facilities Act." It has the effect of making third-party-content websites virtual dumpsters packed full of trash-talking, flaming, and live Google Bomb ordinance. These sites can become cesspools of miscreant deviance bubbling over with poisonous cauldrons spewing hatred and lies. Welcome to Section 230, the veritable poster child for unanticipated consequences.

If you post a rebuttal, it will make the site or page more powerful and relevant in the eyes of Google and the result will be more prominent. It's known as "bumping" a post and you are doing the job of your detractors. You'll find evidence of this tactic online; usually every so often an anonymous coward seems to show up from nowhere and add a comment to a disparaging blog or forum entry, knowing that search engines love fresh content. And don't be fooled by the site that either invites or tries to shame you into responding and defending yourself. No matter how effective your rebuttal may seem to be to you, a response will "bump" the problem into greater prominence and relevance in the search engine results, which then turns your headache into a migraine. This is doubly dangerous since "bumping" the negative information potentially introduces the "Streisand Effect" into the equation, which is something to avoid if at all possible. It is commonly defined as a phenomenon in which an attempt to censor or remove a piece of information on the web backfires, causing greater publicity. It is named after Barbra Streisand, who filed a lawsuit to get aerial photographs of her home removed from the web for privacy and safety reasons. Basically, a group of people gang up on someone and they all start promoting the problem being complained about so that it becomes much more publicized. It once again depends upon a mob mentality for its success. The promotion is typically driven by either the broad republication of the objectionable material and/or attack commentary. But the real trick is that the participants, and they could number into the thousands from all corners of the globe, start linking to each other again and again but with the target's name in the link. They are using "off-page SEO" through links to have Google present the attacks in results when the complaining party's name is searched on Google. Links are some of the most powerful tools used in search engine optimization, so it's no surprise that this works so well. In Streisand's case, the resulting backlash of global commentary caused almost half a million visitors from around the world to peek at the images of her humble abode. The ironic twist is that these free-speech fanatics perceive they are protecting the free flow of information on the web by mounting such an attack, but will have no problem threatening to use a "Streisand" attack in order to discourage, intimidate, and suppress the speech of the party originally aggrieved by misconduct. It's like the neighborhood bullies and thugs sending a very clear message to keep quiet and not speak out.

This is why it is so important to build up defenses online before troubles begin. I'll be showing you how to do that. Some of you will find yourself under serious attack and exposed before that seawall is built, your sand dunes regenerated, or the beach replenished. If that happens, consider getting the expert strategists and tacticians involved before trying to "self-help" yourself by directly engaging with the enemy. If you are going to take up arms in an online neighborhood, be prepared to suffer the slings and arrows of outrageous fortune. Because while you may think you are going to war with body armor you're actually wearing a bright orange sweater . . . with a target on the back. And those online neighbors might just show up with bulldozers.

Obfuscating, Aggregating, and
Deleting as a Pastime

Anonymous Speech

Sue is in such a difficult position because she knows she is being attacked unfairly with lies in a virtual-world assassination. At least she sees what is happening and knows the source. But as she looks around, things are becoming murky. People are jumping into the discussions from all directions, anonymously and with pseudonyms. *Who are these people? And why are they saying these things about me?* At least she knew the identity of her attackers in the beginning. Now, they speak anonymously, constrained not in the least by society's norms and mores of conduct. She is scared of the unknown. She asks herself over and over again: *What right do they have?*

Well, the right to speak anonymously is an important aspect of our right to free speech. Free speech, of course, is wisely protected by the First Amendment. And the Supreme Court has consistently protected the right to anonymous speech . . . *"protections for anonymous speech are vital to democratic discourse."* Today that seemingly sacrosanct right to hide behind anonymity or pseudonyms (assumed names) is becoming more and more at risk. And it should be.

There are a lot of reasons why the Internet should change the Supreme Court's opinion about the sanctity of anonymous speech. Today there is no expense to be incurred in speaking anonymously, the geographic reach of anonymous speech is not merely local but global, the damage capable of being caused by anonymous comments online is greater, the distribution channels are unlimited, the impact of the speech itself can be manipulated by technical methodologies, the recipients of anonymous speech can be artfully controlled and the public benefit diminished, and the true identity of the anonymous speaker can be wiped out of existence in seconds. The day will likely come when the Supreme Court addresses anonymous speech and strips away anonymous-speech rights if things keep going the way they are today.

Many anonymous posters bent on perpetrating online attacks, whether just using the anonymity label or a pseudonym or even an assumed identity, are cowards. They are scared to disclose their identity because they don't have the courage to stand up for their "convictions." And they are scared to get caught. Free anonymous speech is their virtual ski mask as they threaten and rob families and businesses of their livelihoods and good names. Their lawyers will argue that the right to anonymous speech is at the foundation of our country as they point to the Federalist Papers written anonymously by Alexander Hamilton, James Madison, and John Jay in support of the ratification of the U.S. Constitution.

On the other hand, during this same time, fifty-six men signed the Declaration of Independence. Maybe John Hancock just had bad vision, but my guess is that his signature was a courageous statement to all the land that he believed so mightily in the words that he was not afraid to deal with the consequences. What would have become of our founding fathers' dreams if the signatures were of "Julius Caesar," "Genghis Khan," and the eponymous "anonymous"?

Having said all of this, the good news is that **there is no absolute right to online anonymity**. The courts have long recognized the need to unmask those who hide behind false identities on the Internet. Those who defame, those who spam, those who hack, and in some circumstances those who use wrongful commercial speech . . . their anonymity is rarely protected. Every computer or network has an Internet Protocol (IP) address, much like a street address. Legal subpoenas to a website will net the IP address of the offender, and a follow-up subpoena to the Internet Service Provider (ISP) will identify the user of the IP address at the time of the "anonymous speech." This usually works well.

But there are often two practical impediments that could arise in trying to unmask an anonymous speaker. ISPs usually only hold onto their records for short periods of time. This is changing, and there have been efforts in Congress to mandate records retention, probably because a major e-mail provider had a policy of disposing of all records after ninety days and this hampered the prosecution of a 9/11 terrorist mastermind. We should all encourage such legislation.

The other hurdle is more troublesome. The website itself hosting the targeted comments may elect to not keep its records of who visited and what was done. These automatically generated records are known as log files, and many of the public-interest groups openly publish directions on how to get rid of these files and the personally identifiable information that could identify a scofflaw. They even have names for the three techniques recommended: obfuscation, aggregation, and deletion. Nowhere do they mention to their constituents that once notice of a claim that might require the production of such records is received, it is against the law to delete the log files. Some might wonder, as I do, how this endeavor is in the "public interest"?

So what to do? We need Congress to amend Section 230 of the Communications Decency Act to require the complete maintenance of log files indefinitely in order for websites to get immunity. Consider what your Congressman would do if you and yours write a letter and sign it "anonymous," demanding such a change? You'll need the courage to actually lay claim to your communication. But be careful out there. The free-speech expansionists will attack you by inciting their considerable fanatical constituencies to begin a shaming and taint-by-association campaign. Wondering what that might look like? Follow along.

Sue is about to learn all about it.

THE SCARLET LETTER

"Sue Scheff is the biggest fraud there ever was. . . ."

"My family was exploited by PURE and Sue Scheff. . . ."

"Cons like Sue need to be exposed. . . ."

"She places kids in risky programs. . . ."

"I do not want to see children sent to yet another
abusive program at the hands of Sue and P.U.R.E. . . .
I want to be sure they do not fall prey to her. . . ."

"Sue does not know anything about what it means to tell the truth.
A lot of it is about her website and the lies that are found on there.
The lies are related to false advertising. . . ."

"It has to do with her lack of ethics and her lack of professionalism. . . ."

"PURE and Scheff and her associates are crooks. . . .
plain and simple. . . ."

"PURE's behavior puts everyone at risk. I suggest all those
associated with PURE take a step back and reflect!"

"PURE will damage the credibility of anyone
who is associated with them. . . ."

And the hits just keep on coming, folks! When Clark said, "Sue you are going down," it wasn't an idle threat. As for me being scared to death . . . not just yet. But mortified? Humiliated? Angry? You bet. With probably ten other emotions all rolled into the biggest, messiest ball of confusion imaginable.

And there seemed to be nothing I could do about it. *Aw, c'mon, you could have done SOMETHING*, you might be thinking—and as I'm writing this, knowing what I know now . . . I have to remind myself that in 2003 there weren't nearly as many resources available for me to turn to. If only I had known John and had access to his legal smarts. If only I knew then what I know now. If only, if only, if only . . .

Unfortunately I can't turn back the hands of time and do things differently, but what I can do is offer a template of what an online character assassination looks like. It's ugly. But from a distance, and when it's not you, it's rather fascinating, maybe a little shocking, and for those who enjoyed *The Exorcist*, it might even be mildly entertaining. Like a bad car wreck you can't tear your eyes away from.

What's truly awful is that a lot of innocent bystanders get hit along the way. Maybe they're in the passenger seat, trusting you have control of the steering wheel when the tires hit a patch of black ice. Maybe they're well-meaning observers at the initial site of the scene trying to direct traffic. Or could be they're an associate standing too close to the "Information Highway," and if they don't get out of the way and quick—*smack!* They're road kill.

Taint by association. Make no mistake. Even your most trusted allies can come to a point that the instinct for survival overtakes the highest moral ground. Think of it this way: Do you try to save a drowning man going under for the last time or save yourself because he can't swim anyway and the safety of shore is getting further from sight? If you choose the first option, probably neither of you will make it. But if you do the smart thing, as difficult as the decision is to make, at least one of you has a chance of living another day. Besides, there's a spouse and kids and your own business to consider. And, all things considered, only a fool would choose otherwise.

A public shaming has to be one of the worst things anyone can experience, whether it takes place in a small community or on the larger stage of media coverage. But I think what took me aback as my own shaming took off and was propelled into the stratosphere, was not only my lack of ability to defend myself in the court of public opinion, but that the court itself had no checks and balances in place. Even if yellow journalism reeks from a tabloid magazine, there is still a measure of accountability for what's going to print. And since most newspapers try to be careful so the editor doesn't have to print a retraction or make an apology, why shouldn't a website owner be required to maintain some standard of civil discourse, have some responsibility attached to their ownership of a cybernewsstand that's producing written material?

It made no sense to me then and it makes no sense to me now, this absolute free-for-all ability to say virtually anything about anyone without a shred of proof or a drop of truth to it and present it as confirmed fact for all the world to see. But the thing is this: when you're being publicly defamed, you don't want anyone to know, you don't want anyone to see, because not only is it painfully embarrassing, once a lie gets repeated again and again, it starts to have the ring of truth, and if it's starting to make you question yourself then surely others are going to step back and wonder if there just might be a little validity to these accusations after all.

I did not want anyone to know. I didn't want anyone to see. I didn't tell my friends or my family. My sense of humiliation went that deep. The public shaming was doing its job.

As for my job, while I was still getting in my car each morning and driving to my office, my upbeat attitude was replaced with caution, a sense that I needed to keep looking over my shoulder, and a creeping suspicion that the reason my phone wasn't ringing quite as much as usual was because word was spreading within the community that my reputation might not be as sterling as once believed—and remember, this is a community where reputation is *everything* and must be protected at all costs. Since the reputations of your closest associates are just as precious to them as yours is to you, well, better be careful standing too close because this thing could be contagious. After all, who wants to be linked to a scam and have their own credibility kicked into the gutter?

There's no way I could make this stuff up. It's the real deal. Read on:

From Anonymous: "What Steve did was totally fraudulent. Sue played a part in all of this. A significant part, and therefore they both should be held accountable."

Clark responds: "Yes. (What they've done) is called a scam, a scam orchestrated by a group of individuals. People can and should be held accountable for their actions (Steve, Scheff, the Trekkers)."

Who is "Anonymous"? Is it someone I know? And now the Trekkers are being held accountable . . . for what? What did they do besides vote to remove Clark from the group and then try to stick up for me? And she's not through with them yet:

> "I am talking about PURE/Trekkers and those I have had experience with. All they have is each other and the stories they have come up with. If you're (involved with them) I feel sorry for you. They are not honest and truthful people."
>
> **From Anonymous:** "So, it's just the Trekker's that are liars, according to you."
>
> **Clark responds:** "I am saying that Sue/PURE are liars. If you stand by them you stand by liars. That leads me to believe the truth does not matter to you."

Again, who are these anonymous people? Is this the same "Anonymous" or another one? Maybe a different one since this second anon poster doesn't seem as hostile as the first. But then, some more anonymous people show up, piling on the, um, compliments:

> "I think that red sweater (she's wearing) is to set off the fake 'glamour shot photo,' anything to try and make herself look a little bit better. It ALMOST works."

What photo is this person talking about? Are pictures being posted of me on some other website, is there something else happening that I don't know about? And am I starting to show some signs of paranoia? Because I'm looking at this next post from another "Anonymous" who's directly addressing me, as if he/she knows I'm lurking and they're salivating to get in my face:

"Lady, if anyone here needs to think before they speak, it's you—
especially since you're setting yourself out as some caring mom who
just wants to help others. You're withholding truth from people who
trust you. There is no way you're going to convince me that you give
a rat's ass about what happens to someone else's kid. And I hope you
pay for your greediness and pseudo-philanthropy some day."

So…I need to think before I speak around there. But I haven't whispered a word on this website. Is someone else pretending to be me?
Snap out of it, Sue! Get a grip!

And yet, when people who have been in your corner are being
repeatedly warned, "Sue is a problem. She is damaging to our credibility.
People need to be steered away from the controversy that surrounds her.
Anyone who is conversing with her needs to know this. Especially the parents …" Let's just say getting a grip could be a bit more of a challenge
than usual. Especially when parents are making inquiries and are getting responses like this:

> **From Anonymous parent:** "I am looking for a therapeutic board-
> ing school and have heard good things about the work PURE does.
> Am I misled? Help."
>
> **Dysfunction Junction responds:** "Yes, you are SERIOUSLY misled.
> Please have a look at this forum to see what PURE is all about. Well, I'll
> save you some time. It's MONEY. More likely than not, you'll get a
> more f**ked up version back from whatever 'school' in which you
> incarcerate your kid. For your child's sake, ASK QUESTIONS."

Needless to say I didn't get a chance to respond to any questions
the parent might have had to ask.

Besides realizing that my organization was in jeopardy of becoming permanently crippled with the online version of getting kneecapped with a baseball bat, it was becoming increasingly apparent that what started out as some sort of revenge by Clark, then aided by Smith, was gathering a cacophony of voices, many anonymous or pseudonymous, and those voices, while often shrill, had enough intelligence and reason sprinkled in to lend the gathering crowd a certain measure of credibility.

Meanwhile, my own credibility was being brought into question by some of my professional associates. What I did not know at the time, and would later discover from a witness deposition, is that my name was being removed from the Northern California school psychologist referral directory due to the backlash against a therapist who had recommended me many, many times in the past. Apparently one of his clients was doing their homework before contacting me and was appalled to discover that I was a crook and a fraud that exploited families and put children in risky programs. Oh, and since so many people had confirmed my status as a liar who suckered families in with false advertising, anyone who believed a word from the PURE website would do so at their children's expense. And so, as this educational psychologist colleague of mine would later testify, "I immediately stopped referring people to Ms. Scheff and PURE . . . because I felt that it was affecting my credibility if I referred any client to anyone that had so many assailable remarks about their services that were public information."

Are we having fun yet? No? Then let's invite some more VIPs to the party. How about the Broward County PTA? You know, the same county where I live and PURE is based. The same schools where I spent countless hours meeting with guidance counselors and speaking to groups, including of course, PTAs and PTOs.

Not one to be idle, Smith decided to leave a post on the Broward County PTA's discussion board. And what should it be regarding? Have a look:

RE: All snake oil salesmen!
From: (Smith)
Date: 04 Nov
Time: 20:25:04

Comments

I heard that PURE (Sue Scheff) has been recruiting through the Broward County School District. You should know that [redacted] is a part of the PURE network of schools and programs. It's an old, old scam. Seen it many times before. "Experience is that marvelous thing that enables you to recognize a mistake when you make it again."

—*Mark Twain*

Nice. Now Mark Twain gets quoted on recognizing one's mistakes (i.e., stop working with Sue Scheff or you'll be sorry) and Smith gets points for proving she's literate. As for the redacted name of the school she mentioned, it had lost its license due to a tragic occurrence, so what glee she had to take in asserting my advocacy for them. There are just a few hitches:

PURE doesn't own, operate, or manage any schools or programs, so to say we have a "network of schools and programs" is inaccurate since our primary purpose is to distribute information about a variety of programs (the good, the bad, the ugly), whether they pay us for recommending them or not. We never received any money from the program in question; it wasn't even the sort of program we would ordinarily tell a family about. And with regard to that tragic occurrence, PURE had absolutely nothing to do with it, not even remotely, so to directly link us not only to the program but to the reason it was closed down, is such a convoluted twisting of the truth . . . give me a break.

Oh, BTW, I was not alerted to this posting until December 31, 2003. Happy New Year! Looking on the bright side, at least Thanksgiving and Christmas breaks might have slowed down the traffic of visitors to the Broward County PTA's discussion board.

Somewhere in that time frame my unlisted home phone number appeared on Smith's website. It was removed very quickly, almost as soon as I was notified about it by one of my remaining loyalists. But now I had to wonder, *is this now moving to offline, personal attacks on me? Should I be expecting phone calls from this growing mass of detractors? What's going to happen next?*

Several situations did arise to indicate the sown seeds of distrust were finding fertile ground. There was a story on my website that a young lady had submitted about her own experience in a program. Mary, as I'll refer to her since she is a minor whose name should not be brought into this mess, contacted me one day and asked me to remove her contribution. Which I did, no questions asked. Maybe a few weeks had passed when she got in touch again and apologized, saying her decision had been wrong and I could re-post her story if I so wished. She seemed upset and I didn't want to press her on the details, but I had an idea who might be behind this and decided to do a little investigating on Smith's website to see what I could turn up from the forum.

I didn't know exactly what I was looking for but it didn't take me long to find the "Ah-hah!" piece of evidence . . . which is now reserved for posterity as Exhibits 3 and 4 of the trial exhibits. It seems that Clark decided to take it upon herself to send a personal e-mail to this young person, then proudly posted her handiwork on the open forum—along with the girl's response. Starting from the bottom of the thread and working up, here goes:

"Hi Mary. I am the mother of the boys who were at the school in Costa Rica. I am writing to you because I saw that you posted on Sue Scheff's website. I want you to know that your creditability (sic) will be lost because of your association with her. She knows nothing about children and how to address their needs. The schools she places kids in are unregulated. So being associated with Sue is very dangerous."

Clark then posts Mary's private reply:

"Thank you for the advice and I appreciate it. I will definitely not associate with her anymore and try to take the story off her web. —Mary"

And then one of my defenders, someone from the Trekkers, responded:

"Mary took her story off PURE because YOU harassed her to."

To which Clark shot back:

"First of all I did not harass her to do so. I simply told her Sue was very much one to be avoided, given her profession and all. Why do you people keep making this up? You make constant accusations that are so far from the truth. Learn to be more careful about what you say and what you accuse people of, then maybe someone will believe you."

Okay, just so we can make things more complicated than they already are, Mary had been involved with a film in production that dealt with the stories of teens abused in boot camps. I was not involved with the film in any way, but they had a link to PURE's "Helpyourteens.com" on their website since I had established a reputation as a trustworthy resource for parents of teens that needed information on effective and safe programs.

Having dealt with Mary, Clark decided to follow up with the director of the film, who we will call Bill. It didn't take much digging on my part to become privy to the private correspondence between him and Clark since, again, it was posted on the open forum. Here 'tis:

"Dear Bill,

You are going to have some problems on your hand with Mary and her association with your film. She is affiliated with Sue Scheff of PURE, Inc. Anyone who is affiliated with her will be found not creditable (sic).
—M. Clark"

"Ms. Clark,

Mary is in no way associated with Sue Scheff. They have corresponded in the past, but have no affiliation whatsoever. We have done due diligence on Mary and she is an advocate of teens and stopping the abuse. I can't discuss it in any greater detail, but rest assured we are doing our best to have the utmost integrity with our film. FYI: the link to Help Your Teens is coming down until we can investigate it further.

Thanks so much.
—Bill"

Clark then goes on to announce to the forum at large:

> "Now if you look at the time on Mary's e-mail it was before I spoke
> with the director of the movie. I believe my speaking with both of
> them played a part in the removal of Mary's letter from the PURE, Inc.
> website."

I suppose this was a major victory for Clark. She was able to dis-
credit me to someone else and get my link removed from their website. But I was still left with the never-ending question of: *Why? What
was driving her to ruin me? Could someone actually hold this much of a grudge
for getting kicked off of a private listserv?* She seemed to be feeding off the
energy I was being drained of, and while she showed no signs of
remorse for her infliction of injury on another human being, I didn't
think she was crazy. This was all so calculated, so precise, like a surgeon wielding a cyberscalpel to eviscerate a living person minus anes-
thesia. Cruel? Yes. But it was more like being attacked by a master of
mind games than the Mad Hatter.

I, on the other hand, had begun to suffer some emotional fallout. I
wasn't able to sleep. I was starting to cry a lot in private. The smile
that had been so quick before had become strained and forced when
I attended meetings or public events. I wasn't hard-pressed to force
too many smiles since my invitations were drying up.

I knew that if this didn't stop soon—and things certainly didn't
seem to be heading in that direction—I would have no choice but to
do . . . something. What, I didn't know, but I realized the situation was
approaching critical mass. After all, when I counted my blessings, I
was sincerely grateful that at least my membership hadn't been revoked
at the Better Business Bureau.

Flu Shots Don't Work After You Have the Flu

Search Engines as Reputation Engines

What Sue is quickly finding out is that Google is not only the leading search engine, it is the dominant and most trusted reputation engine. That means that someone doing research on a subject or looking you up will go to the Google search engine and see what everyone else is saying about an industry or you. As an individual, you should be protecting your personal name. As a business, you should be protecting your business brand as well as the reputation of individuals important to your business, like owners and executives. For most people, Google will be the only reputation engine you need to worry about. The ten results that come up on the first page are by far the most important. But even one negative result could offset the goodwill generated from the other nine positive results. So the challenge for individuals, small businesses, and the Fortune 500 is to control the first page of Google results as a starting point. Results on other pages are important, although most people only view the first page of results.

But think about it. The nature of the search will define the scope of reputation influence. If you are researching the name of your brain surgeon, you will go very deep in results, maybe even twenty-five pages. If you are checking out your hairdresser, a quick look at the first page of results may suffice. And motivation matters; if you have someone who is really looking to get you, that person's search will likely become very extensive in seeking out online skeletons in your closet for cannon fodder. Sue is beginning to see the impact of false and negative information online. These attackers are hurting her business in more ways than one: they are trying to ruin her reputation so that prospective clients will just take a pass on her business; they are going to community organizations and third parties and striking at the foundations of her credibility; and they are campaigning to cut off her source of referrals, a critical component in just about any business involved in counseling and the medical industry.

I've seen many people fret about a damaging comment made online that will likely never show up toward the top of Google results. Generally you don't need to sweat that. In fact, if you do, it could gain attention, create "piling on," and allow the post to morph into something that really does gain traction and show up high in Google results.

There are many websites that can create problems for your name and reputation, and each has to be dealt with on a one-off basis. If you sell on eBay you know about its reputation rating system. Amazon has one too. If you are in the travel industry, you are likely familiar with the leading rating services for hotels, resorts, and the like. There are websites that serve as clearinghouses for reporting purported rip-offs and scams. And in Sue's case, she is dealing with a "review site" that is industry specific. If you are concerned enough to want to address everything said on the web about you, then there are reputation monitoring and management companies that can be helpful (we'll discuss this at more length later), and can range significantly in cost from a modest fee up to $10,000 per month for their services, depending on your needs. Be forewarned that you will soon find out that it is impossible to totally control your online image. But there are ways to approach false and defamatory attacks, gross privacy violations, and other related damaging information with or without the help of a reputation-management firm.

Deciding on how to approach the problem of being exposed to attacks online is a lot like dealing with the flu. You'll decide for yourself whether taking that flu shot is a wise choice. You'll decide your avoidance tactics when that friend of yours gets sick. And as the flu bug moves closer and closer to home, you'll decide when to act, if at all. When you wake up with that uneasy feeling, you'll wonder whether to go to the doctor or just visit your local pharmacy. If you're thinking ahead, you'll just go to your medicine cabinet. How you deal with work as your energy level diminishes, and what part of the bed looks most comfortable as the battle rages within you, are your decisions to make. In the aftermath, you'll decide what balls have been dropped and the pace and order of picking those up.

And so it is with managing the health of your online reputation.

The good news is whether you are proactive and decide to build up your defenses in advance, are vigilant in monitoring your environment, or are trying to deal with an existing attack, the tactics and tools are, for the most part, the same. The difference is in the timing. Flu shots don't work after you have the flu. So if you get sick, no matter how hard you may have tried to avoid it, you can use the same techniques to begin to combat the effects. Consider this guidance the contents of your virtual medicine chest. There is rarely a cure, but the effects can be managed. Obviously the best approach is to be well rested and healthy so you can avoid illness or curtail the duration and severity of the effects. Let's start out with discovering the symptoms . . . and the early warning system you can put into place to tip you off that a problem is on the horizon.

Before we do so, remember the way things used to be. Community gossip is very frustrating because it is almost impossible to deal with early. The falsehoods are whispered behind your back, out of earshot, and you are often the last to know because your friends don't want to embarrass you. Not so on the web, thank goodness. Because with the open flow of information comes . . . well . . . the open flow of information. We are dealing with a two-sided sword and it cuts both ways. So you can easily set up an early notification system yourself in minutes to let you know whenever your name is mentioned online. Sue didn't do that, and she is suffering the consequences. Or you can get more extensive monitoring of your name with a number of reasonably priced commercial solutions. Even the World Bank offers a reputation monitoring system for free. And unlike the flu shot, you don't have to leave home, there is no risk of adverse reaction, and no needles are involved.

And, by the way, you'll find my thoughts on how you can immediately initiate your very own early warning system in the next section. It's really quite simple.

When the Water Is Receding, It's Too Late

Your Early Warning System

Sir Winston Churchill once said that "[a] lie gets halfway around the world before the truth has a chance to get its pants on."

Let's first appreciate how much more quickly information flows today. Churchill was surely making the point that timely intelligence is critical. Fortunately, we can serve as our own intelligence agency by using free and easily implemented tools available to everyone with computer access. It is critically important that you get as much warning as possible of the beginning of a problem so you can prevent small annoyances from becoming full-blown mobosphere attacks. Everyone needs to be putting together an early warning system.

Remember the horrible sight of the waters receding far out to sea as the devastating Indian Ocean tsunami approached the beaches in 2004? Of course it was too late to build a seawall, reinforce the concrete in the buildings, or even prevent the outdoor furniture from becoming missiles. Some of the lucky ones were able to make a run for it and escape. But for many more who continued to frolic in the shallow waters, the vision of this strange occurrence meant it was simply too late. Let's be clear; this devastating and heartwrenching loss of life cannot be compared to anything we discuss in this book. But it should serve as a stark and tragic reminder that disasters do happen and can come with no warning. And it can serve as a call to action for you. Don't take a wait-and-see attitude with your online reputation. The first wave will come out of the blue, the second and third will gain power, and it will be too late to escape.

Back in 2003, at the beginning of Sue's problems, sneak attacks were not only possible, but prevalent. Today Sue has access to a broad range of tools, some of which existed in Sue's prewar years, and others that have arisen since then. If you take my advice, the likelihood of a Pearl Harbor-like sneak attack will be far less. It's safe to say that in the past six years the web has come a long way in allowing you to build up both effective defenses and a robust early warning system.

There are three primary things you have to be concerned about online. The first is the use of your name. The second is the use of your content. The third is the use of your site or web property by hackers. Obviously the use of your name is of paramount concern and will be the primary purpose of implementing an early warning system. But copyright and hacking issues are worth dealing with also at the same time, and do have some pertinence to online attacks against you and yours.

The three leading search engines are Microsoft, Yahoo, and Google. Each offers an "Alert" service. This means that you can ask a search engine to tell you whenever your name is mentioned. Put your name in as an alert on the simple online form, with your e-mail address, and you'll get an e-mail whenever that search engine runs across your name. Register on all three search engines, but the most important is Google. Remember, Google is *the* reputation engine, the dominant search engine, and the one you have to worry about the most. If Google doesn't find an attack coming at you, far more often than not you need not worry.

In order to set up a Google Alert, just go to the page *(www.google.com/ alerts)* and familiarize yourself with the process. It is simple. Use quotation marks around your search term for an "exact" match. Otherwise, you'll get a lot of trash coming at you. Get your feet wet first, set up several alerts, see how

the process works and go from there. The same general process can be followed for the other search engines. And you might as well set up a Twitter
alert while you are at it. The Twitter site does not offer this service so go to
Twilert.com to set it up or another independent site offering this free service.
Then you'll know whenever your name shows up in a "tweet" and you can
read what was said about you.

Note that you usually set the frequency of receipt of e-mail alerts. Be careful with this . . . you want to know about a problem but not be unduly bur-
dened with a lot of interruptions. When you do get an e-mail alert, open it,
review the results, and click on the link and investigate the page content. If
you do not want the website to know of your visit, you can use an anonymizer
service that changes your unique Internet address (known as Internet Protocol or IP address). Even with an anonymizer, don't make the mistake of believing that you are omnipotent. The web is not anonymous. No matter how often
you hear that it is, remember that it is not. The young man who allegedly
hacked Sarah Palin's e-mail account used an anonymizer, but the FBI quickly
asked for, and got, the real user's identity.

Once you have set up your alerts on the names you want to monitor, you
may decide to keep an eye on your website content to make sure no one is
stealing it. Content is often stolen as part of an attack and used in a number
of ways. If your site is duplicated (it only takes seconds to do that by copying
the publicly available computer code on your web pages) then your business
or web properties could be targeted for destruction. A duplicate site often
replaces the original site in Google's search results, which means your attacker
will be sitting in that nice position you have built up over the years and redirecting traffic. We've even seen instances of someone stealing our client's website content only to publish allegations that our client was the thief of his
content. Coupled with a call to action by the real thief, this type of a tactic can
lead to attacks of all sorts coming at you.

You should take a unique phrase from your website and add it to the search engine alert service just as you did with your name. And if you find someone has stolen your content, Google has a reporting system for just such situations. Go to its site and submit the notification. And to cover more extensive websites with many pages, you'll find inexpensive commercial solutions online, like Copyscape and Copysentry (www.copyscape.com), that function much like the alert systems of search engines but with some bells and whistles.

The last use I want to mention for the search engine alerts is an early warning hacking alert. Hacking is the most uncommon attack tactic, but is often the most effective because it is the "silent killer" . . . you don't know what is happening, but your web properties are being seen by Google unfavorably and your rankings in natural results are dropping into oblivion. Some of Sue's sites recently underwent a hack attack in which a very advanced virus was planted. As litigation lawyers chasing the bad guys, Dozier Internet Law comes under attack often. In one instance, a hacker got into our website and posted child porn and then began claiming our firm was distributing child pornography. In another attack the same day, a Britney Spears video was uploaded into our administrative area of one section of our site, and the website crashed when the hacker activated hundreds of computer servers worldwide to play the video simultaneously. And every year in August, when the hackers of the world go to their "underground" annual convention (DEF-CON) in Las Vegas, Dozier Internet Law has a huge spike in hacker intrusion attempts.

We learned our lesson after the first incident and upgraded our security dramatically. But you likely won't have the level of protection necessary to keep a hacker out of your website unless you are operating on a high security e-commerce platform. Now that you understand a bit of the hacking landscape, you can see how dangerous hacks into your site can be. But you can't use the search engine alerts to deal with these. There are commercial products and services for security monitoring available but no easy and free solution.

So, while the risk of hackers attacking you in many ways exists, there is only one type of hacking that can be disclosed by use of the alerts. It's the use of your site to facilitate spam. Think of this as a hijacking for commercial purposes. This type of hack fills two purposes. The first is to hijack your site's reputation and authority and the second is to make a quick buck before the hack is disclosed. But now that you appreciate the risks, you can use the alert to combat the growing problem of hackers who are accessing your site and launching a landing page for spam campaigns and making you look like a spammer. If you don't catch it quickly, you could end up being on spam blacklists, be listed on major spam reporting sites, and have Google disqualify your website from being listed in results. So go into your junk e-mail account, look at the most prominent spam solicitations you are receiving, and set up an alert with your domain name and the spam product or service name. If your website is abcdef.com, and you are getting a lot of spam pushing online casinos, just put in as search alert terms "abcdef.com online casino." (Do not enter the quotation marks when you set this up or you will only get alerts for an exact match of the terms in that order, which means you'll likely never get an alert.) If you are ever hacked, immediately contact your webhost and report it to Google. Have your webhost clear out any links or other goodies the hacker left behind. And make sure the hole the hackers exploited is patched. Google is predicting that this type of situation will be a huge issue beginning in 2009.

Also, Technorati.com has an extensive searchable database of blog entries that is a handy source for seeing what is being said about you in the blogosphere, and the inventory of content included on Technorati is often more complete than any of the search engines. This resource should be part of your ongoing early warning alert system.

A tool worth mentioning is Backtype.com. You can register for free and get alerts sent to you when comments in blogs show up mentioning your name. So if you put your name in for an alert, you'll know when a comment is made about you, and you can go see all of the comments made by the same person. If you want to keep an eye on a particular person you can simply set up an alert for that name and have a virtual private eye reporting his every move in the blogosphere. Obviously this adds an important tool to your arsenal since you can literally follow your attacker around the web and glean all kinds of good information about what might be coming next.

Finally, don't forget that there are plenty of free online resources that will let you monitor the online world. You can get an alert for every change to web-page content. If you are being attacked on a particular site, or just have suspicions something bad may be coming, you can stay abreast of developments without having to visit the site. Don't keep visiting the site. The website owner often watches his log files and will know when you are visiting and what you are looking at. The last thing you want to do is give the scofflaw a reason to gloat and escalate his attacks.

Stay aware. Understand where your web traffic is coming from. If you have a blog, check out the sites sending traffic to you. This is a great way of identifying the source of referrals. If your attacker is linking to your blog, you'll find out pretty quickly when traffic starts flowing.

I would be remiss if I did not let you know that many of these alert systems will not function at all if the website is not indexed by the search engines. I have seen attack websites that are virtually underground and the content will never show up on search engines or in alerts. All that is required is the use of a "robots.text" file, which prohibits the little computer programs called robots or spiders from entering the site to record the content. This is rarely an issue since the purpose of attacks is most often to disparage your online reputation by getting Google to search and index the site. But if you run into one of these situations, you don't really need to worry about an early warning system anyway. You are being targeted in a big way. Call your lawyer.

If you are ready to jump in feet first with everything you've got, there are other online solutions for reputation-management monitoring that may be worthy of your consideration. You'll need to decide on the size and power of the early warning system you require. Don't try to kill a fly with a sledgehammer, and don't go hunting elephants with a BB gun.

In retrospect, Sue could have set up many of these warning systems and seen the waves of attacks approaching far in advance, which, perhaps, could have enabled her to nip this in the bud with a well-placed telephone call or two. Maybe she could have gone to her important business partners and sources of credibility and referrals and spun the coming attacks to minimize the impact. Aggressive and timely SEO and reputation-management strategies could have been initiated. There are so many possible approaches that could have prevented the escalation of the attacks. Or at least limited their impact. But instead, frozen with self-doubt and fear, she stood on the beach, mesmerized by this odd occurrence, soon to be greeted by an online tsunami that would devastate her.

The Land of a Million Dreams

Product and Service Review Websites

On a recent trip with my boys to Disney World we couldn't resist a day in Magic Kingdom and found ourselves in Tomorrowland. We went through the Carousel of Progress and saw what the future would look like in years to come. Much of it was vaguely familiar. Then we took a boat ride through It's A Small World, and again I had the feeling of déjà vu all over again.

As we were heading home that evening we learned that both of those attractions had first appeared at the New York World's Fair in 1964. And memories came flowing back to me about that summer in '64 when my family packed up and took off to "see the future" in New York City. It struck me that only in Disney World could a view of the future be a trip back in time. Unfortunately, unlike our latest victorious sports heroes, who always seem to be "going to Disney World" as they walk off the field, my comments won't be taking you to Disney World any time soon. And we already know that yesterday was not tomorrow. Living in the past will bring nothing but headaches.

Sue comes from the time years ago when the way of checking out a business's reputation was to pull a Dun & Bradstreet credit report, inquire about its Better Business Bureau (BBB) record, and check with licensing agencies and trade references. For individuals, pulling a report from one of the three major credit bureaus coupled with former employer and personal references was the extent of due diligence. For products, one might turn to *Consumer Reports*.

All of these reference points of contact have a lot of checks and balances in place. A BBB complaint can be dealt with by resolving the dispute and turning it overnight into a positive. A negative item on a credit report can be challenged and unless verified within thirty days it will be removed courtesy of the Fair Credit Reporting Act. *Consumer Reports* relies on scientific analyses and exceptional editorial judgment and discretion. Employers have all kinds of privacy policy restrictions in place today and rarely give a negative review of a former employee. Licensing agencies, often run by the state, were never really very good at responding with up-to-date information and often required an inconvenient personal visit to the most congested area of town. And those trade and personal references supplied by the party you are checking up on? Come on, everyone picks out references they know will offer glowing praise.

Almost all of these aggregators of reputation information were complaint-based and not anonymous. If a business reported a delinquency to the credit bureau, or a license agency undertook an investigation, or the

BBB opened up a complaint, these weren't based on their crack team of investigators beating the bushes to find the dissatisfied or disenfranchised. The information was based upon a complaint from a real, live person. You had to really be pissed off to go through the hassle of identifying yourself and filing a complaint, knowing in all likelihood it would never see the light of day or lead toward a resolution.

Today, as Sue has come to realize, things have changed. Complaints are openly solicited, websites offer simple, easy, and free ways to file a very serious complaint, the comments often become highly visible in days, and this will often lead to a dialogue and resolution. And for that, we owe our thanks to the online world. If only it were that simple and ended there. If only people could refrain from misusing these reputation aggregators. But they can't. So scam reporting websites that were conceived as public service sites have become venues used by your competitor or ex-girlfriend to anonymously make you the target of the day. And Sue is still today dealing with the backlash of attacks that started on an industry-specific consumer review site that at one time may have been a consumer protector but turned into a vindictive persecutor.

There are generally three types of scam reporting websites. The first is the type of site Sue has been dealing with, one that seems to have come into existence to expose a specific industry's abuses. These are specialized complaint sites that really are not professional in appearance or function but can offer valuable information. Often they end up being consumed by negative commentary that grows into outright defamatory attacks and more.

The second is the review website, which when legitimate, welcomes both positive and negative commentary. Honest sites might include Epinions.com, Buzzillions.com, or Mpire.com. These are "product review" sites set up and controlled by disinterested third parties and typically offer reasonably objective and accurate assessments, both good and bad. The more nefarious review websites are owned and controlled by the product owner or an affiliate marketer of one of the products under review. Today these types of sites are widely used by the online nutraceutical (unregulated nutritional "pharmaceuticals" that are all the rage today) industry to offer praise of their own products and criticism of competing products. But they are also gaining popularity along many lines as a seemingly undetectable way of illegally attacking competitors.

The third type of site is the open "free-for-all" consumer protection site like the Better Business Bureau on steroids. The motivations for such sites vary. Niche site owners are usually just craving recognition, power, or attention. At least that is my experience. On the other extreme, the true scam reporting websites like Ripoffreport.com, Complaints.com, and Scam.com have business models. In other words, they make money. Some of them make lots of money. And the more complaints they get, the more money they make. As I write this, Scam.com and Complaints.com are making money through the Google AdSense program. They get paid every time someone clicks on an advertisement. So, if your business is being attacked, and someone is searching for you, the "scam" label could very well show up on the first page of results. Of course the result will be clicked on, and lead to a page tearing into your business. But that is not the worst of it. At the top and along the side of the attack commentary are advertisements. FOR YOUR COMPETITORS!

Driving the profitability of these sites is the new process of online search through which reputation information is gathered. You own a small business, and you want to open a bank account. If your small business is checked out for creditworthiness and you have a couple of delinquencies and an unpaid invoice and big loans on everything, the bank may put in certain restrictions to assure you are fiscally responsible with them. If you are applying for a mortgage, you'll get one, just on more expensive terms. At least that was the way things used to be until the mortgage meltdown. Now imagine that bank and mortgage company checking you out online, and seeing false claims that you are a convicted swindler, use a bunch of aliases, beat your wife, and run a "scam" business that is a front for the mob. All completely fabricated. But that doesn't matter because you won't have a chance of getting a loan or opening a bank account.

But things get worse. Because the scam reporting and dishonest review websites are megamachines soliciting complaints across the web, they are aggregating defamatory attacks at one location and creating a report card featuring all failing grades. Just as problematic, though, is the fact that attacks carried out through these sites are higher profile and more inclined to reach the top of Google's results because the sites themselves are seen by Google as highly authoritative. It's the credit bureau model all over again, aggregating reputation information at one source, but the information at the scam reporting and scam review site is often a bunch of incorrect, false, malicious charges being submitted anonymously from all over the world, rather than relatively reliable and accurate data flowing from identified businesses governed by a very strict federal law. And how does the granddaddy of them all, Ripoff report.com, generate income? It offers to help a business manage the false attacks on its website for a very hefty monthly fee.

That's the fundamental problem with things today. We have the Fair Credit Reporting Act and business policies and practices in place to make sure traditional reputation resources, like the three credit bureaus and credit scoring providers, contain or use only reliable and accurate information. Yet at the same time the most impactful and least reliable source of information about you or your business is governed by no laws or societal norms or mores to protect you. In fact, just the opposite is true. Our laws discourage corrections since Section 230 of the Communications Decency Act (CDA) motivates many sites to simply take the safe route to complete immunity from liability and follow a "no edit" practice. If the content is posted, many sites won't touch it at all, except in situations that implicate child pornography or other clearly criminal activity. As I have said before, this law alone is responsible for most of the published defamation online today because it strips the power to self-regulate and self-police from the website owner. Try to reconcile this approach with the legislative mandates by which the credit bureaus must operate. You can't.

My opinion is that these scam review sites have legal problems, particularly in the trademark infringement arena. But to be fair, the public-interest groups and free-speech expansionists, together with other like-minded and very vocal law professors who reside in the ivory towers of Berkeley and Harvard and that place called self-delusion, believe these scam reporting websites are simply exercises of free speech and fair use rights. The courts haven't gotten around to dealing with this in a detailed and informed way yet. But they will. And my prediction will be that the forces defending Section 230 of the CDA will one day regret that, when given the opportunity, they did not seek a balanced and fair solution. I am reminded of the judge who looked at my opponent over twenty years ago and proclaimed that "[Y]ou live by the sword, you die by the sword" as he found in my client's favor.

If you ever see your name show up on a Google result with one of these scam reporting sites as the source, or you get an alert and you realize these sites are carrying the attack, be very careful. Keep in mind that some are becoming very well camouflaged as they are "outed" and their racket becomes known. But more and more competitors are launching "review sites" that are biased and disparage competing products. We have even found independent sites whose advertisers never seem to get the negative comments. But the non-advertisers get nailed constantly. Basically the source of attacks on your products, services, family, business, and organization can come from so many places that are havens for breeding scofflaw attacks that it is becoming really hard to figure out. You need to be careful because these can be very powerful sites. Whatever your problem is can become much worse overnight, and addressing problems coming from attacks on scam reporting or review websites requires a good deal of finesse and experienced judgment to manage this high-risk environment.

Yes, we live in a new time. It's now a small world, to be sure. And we are all on the rapidly evolving carousel of progress. Learn to adapt to the new world and embrace the nuances of the online business world.

In the meantime, take a look at the Pinocchian ways of these "public interest" groups protecting the scoundrels that attack, rob, and steal. They live in fantasyland, work in yesterdayland, and vacation in wonderland. They offer Mickey Mouse musings, Daffy Duck diatribes, and Goofy grousings in Chicken Little legal briefs, all with the flair and pirate aplomb of a Jack Sparrow. I doubt if they are on the way to Disney World either . . . but they should be . . . it's the land of a million dreams.

All the News That's Fit to Print

Communications Indecency Act

How could this be happening? Why are these problems unique to the online world? We've had newspapers and magazines around for years. It makes no sense. Those are some of the questions going through Sue's mind as she sees site after site willingly host and support the outright lies aimed at her. Ironically, in a rush to protect ISPs, Congress brought it on itself.

Laws come from a lot of different places. Here in the United States, your local city counsel may pass a law. Or your state's legislature can act. As the federal executive branch likes to point out, Congress proposes laws. And thePresident disposes of them. Many come from our English ancestors, and they are part of a body of laws called "common law." These are laws based upon common sense. I guess Congress's laws might be viewed in history as "uncommon nonsense." I'm not sure about that, but for our purposes, it applies. Here's why.

Centuries ago, when scriveners would still turn a simple sentence into an absurdly long soliloquy (they were paid by the word) everyone understood that falsehoods could get you in trouble. The English decided that a publisher of such lies would be liable for damages. The fellow passing out those pamphlets on the corner can't claim he just found them and did not know the author and therefore escape responsibility. Newspapers and magazines that later evolved would, in fact, have a legal obligation to get their facts straight. This made perfect sense. In fact, it became our law in the United States. "Publisher liability," which is the doctrine establishing legal responsibility by a publisher for the contents of a book, magazine, or newspaper, keeps our reporters, editors, and publishers honest. And that law certainly contributed to the public perception that "if it is in the newspaper it must be true."

But along came 1996, the very infancy of the commercialization of the Internet. In the early days, the web was seen primarily as a more effective distribution system. It was easier to shop, easier to research, and you could even send e-mail. It was also the year credit card security became of age and e-commerce platforms began safely processing credit cards. I recall this as an evolutionary moment since my venture-backed e-commerce business I had begun in 1994 could now offer our major financial clients like American Express, Citicorp, and Sears a more robust transaction processing solution. But securely moving financial data over the web was still just a new way of distributing money from customers to merchants and banks. Today, a primary value of the web is the ability to build neighborhoods and communities and interact socially. So by the turn of the century, blogs were evolving, and it wouldn't be long before social networks and video sites boomed as the era of "user-generated content" exploded. Soon, anyone who had anything to say could say it. And in less than ten years the entire landscape of the web had changed from a business-based platform driven by dis-intermediation (taking out the middle man in a transaction) and faster and easier information-distribution systems to a social phenomenon that has changed life as we live it.

In 1995, a court decided that Prodigy, a sort of value-added and private ISP, may have "publisher liability" for statements carried on its online service. So Congress intervened and passed Section 230 of the Communications Decency Act because it did seem fundamentally unfair to apply a doctrine of responsibility to a technology company that had no role in the content. You wouldn't sue the phone company for what happened in a private telephone conversation, it was argued, and at the time it may have made sense to pass Section 230. The goal was to make sure this new thing called the Internet could thrive and grow without undue interference. This was a time when domain names were pretty darn expensive, websites were relatively costly, Google wasn't around, and social networks and blogs were a mere glimmer in someone's eye. So as Congress surveyed the landscape, the law may have made a lot of sense given the landscape of that day.

Little did they know or understand what was to come: free websites, two-dollar domain names, and platforms ready-made for every Larry, Curly, and Moe to launch attacks. You can have your own blog for free today in minutes. And Google came along and nearly cornered the market for online searches. Needless to say, the landscape has changed dramatically. And yet the same law exists in its original form.

More than a dozen years later there remains a law in place that, as we have discussed, dissuades website owners from self-policing and editing away horrible lies and attacks. In other words, the law put into place to protect service providers actually promotes defamation and meaningfully discourages self-regulation and self-policing of the web by the very websites used by scofflaws to carry out their attacks

Here's a quick example. Someone falsely says you are a thief and a wife beater on a forum. You find out about this and send an e-mail to the website owner saying that this guy on your forum is posting outrageous and false lies. If the website pulls it down, and the editing is determined by a court to have materially changed the meaning of the content, then the website owner can be sued. At the least, editing opens up a door for expensive litigation, the last thing a small website owner would want or be able to afford. So, what do you think happens? Defamatory statements rarely get removed from the web by the website owner, even when the desire to do so exists. As we saw earlier, the rule of unintended consequences rears its ugly head.

The body of law dealing with Section 230 is evolving. Judges are disagreeing as to the interpretations of "editing" and when immunity should be awarded. Lawyers debate the issues and disagree. How can we expect a small business person running a website to risk losing everything by trying to navigate through this minefield?

There are ways to solve this problem and actually empower and allow websites, search engines, ISPs, forums, blogs, and the like to self-police and self-regulate without fear of being responsible for something they do not control. Section 230 should be amended so it works to protect legitimate business interests and empowers the web to self-police. Sue must be wondering why her freedom to speak is under direct attack, her freedom to avoid outrageously false attacks on her reputation is being eroded, and her freedom to maintain her reputation and honor as a true measure of the quality of her work is being dismantled. What has happened to the concept of the sanctity of one's reputation? Have we devolved back into the days in which the only way to save your name is a virtual duel? A duel with an interesting choice of weapons: a flame thrower for the attacker, and a pen knife for the attacked?

As the attacks on Sue escalate, there becomes an imbalance between the property and privacy rights of an individual and the rights of the public to know. Rule by the masses and mobs are beginning to control the reputation and honor of Sue. The intellectual justification for an overly protective view of free speech—that truth will win out in an unfiltered marketplace of ideas and therefore free speech must be protected over individual rights—is being revealed as more of a nightmare than an aspirational dream. And in the light of day, the very notion should become a distant figment of our imagination as Sue's right to privacy is invaded. All the news that's fit to print?

Hardly.

DIG A MOAT OR A GRAVE

In order for the next part of my saga to make sense (as if ANY of it makes sense), I need to expand upon something I brought up in the first chapter: how my daughter was abused in a program for at-risk teens, which I removed her from, and subsequently established PURE as a resource for families dealing with this sensitive issue.

I put our story on PURE's website. A cautionary tale to be sure, and all of it was proven to be true. The owners of the very large and powerful Utah-based corporation that oversaw the program my daughter had attended took exception to me taking our experience public. Ironically, I was the one being accused of defamation and they decided to sue *me*. They lost; I won. They appealed; I won again.

I expand on all this in my book *Wit's End*, but don't want to go into any real detail here, except for a few key overlapping issues that directly bear on this story.

First, remember when Clark initially contacted me for help in removing her sons from the Costa Rica program, and I then gave her Steve's contact information for potential assistance? The program her sons were in was owned by the same corporation that ran yet another program, the one I had removed my daughter from. This probably had something to do with the empathy I had when Clark called me up in distress.

Although she repeatedly claimed her family had suffered dramatically from the program she removed her sons from, she testified under oath that she asked the corporation's lawyers for $30,000 to let them access her computer, which supposedly contained correspondence that would be damaging to me. She further testified that she took $12,500 for allowing the lawyers to borrow said computer, which they flew from Utah to Louisiana to personally pick it up.

Nothing damaging surfaced to incriminate me, by the way, but this exchange of money for information transpired in late 2003. The actual details of amounts and arrangements weren't immediately known to me, but Clark made no attempt to hide the exchange, going so far as to post this on Smith's website that December:

> "Somewhere in another thread I told ya'll I would give [redacted] my e-mails. So why you're now surprised I did, I don't understand. I could have said no and had them subpoenaed or I could attempt to negotiate with them and have them pay for them. After all, I incurred a lot of expense removing my boys from a program that I did not want them in. I chose the latter. If you have a problem with that ... well, it's your problem."

Now the third and last point that plays into this unfolding *Twilight Zone* scene is that I had to give a deposition in the case. A very long deposition that weighed in at over 600 pages. And in those pages I was asked about the parents I worked with, their names, and what facilities their teens went to, descriptions of allegations of abuse suf-

fered by children in various programs, and other privileged information concerning many families that I would never reveal to an outside source but was compelled to disclose. There was, however, a
protective order signed by the federal district court judge mandating
that ". . . any names or organizations disclosed in Sue Scheff's deposition, or in future depositions, are subject to this protective order
and may not be disclosed or used outside this litigation."

In addition to this professional probing, I was asked some deeply
personal questions, which I answered. Many of them revolved around
my children, including my daughter's emotional struggles, my son's
learning disability, and much, much more. There were extended
family inquiries, which I answered, regarding my father, my mother,
even my cousin, their addresses, occupations, and financial situations.
Details about my marriage, my divorce, personal finances, and work
history were thoroughly questioned—and answered. And then such
basics as my home address, unlisted phone number, and Social Security number were committed to deposition print.

The final result was far more detailed and graphic than this Cliffs-
Notes version might suggest, basically exposing every particle of my
personal life in stark black-and-white. It left me feeling extremely vulnerable, like some specimen being examined under a microscope and
then dissected in one of those biology classes where the frog gets
pithed.

Well, guess what just happened to show up in Clark's mailbox,
shortly after she turned her computer over to the corporation's
lawyers so they might examine the correspondence she and I had earlier exchanged? And what an inconvenient truth that the judge had
signed off on a protective order to legally shield innocent families
and their children from public exposure, their identities in my

deposition to be revealed ONLY in this litigation. Huh. That's interesting. There were only two law firms litigating the case last I'd checked, and it's sure hard to imagine my own attorney finagling a copy of my deposition into Clark's possession.

Still, as Clark would later testify, she had no idea who had sent her my deposition; it simply showed up in her mailbox without a return address.

What magic! Amazing! Lance Burton, David Copperfield: *move over.*

So, do you care to hazard a guess as to what comes next?

Ah, there's nothing quite like having selected portions of one's deposition posted on an open Internet forum. Not all of the best juicy bits, mind you—at least, not yet—but definitely some private information that was not meant for public consumption. To say I was horrified would be an understatement. Especially when a flurry of posts between Smith and Clark made it clear they intended to post my *entire* deposition on the website. There was just one little impediment they were trying to work out: Smith as the website administrator had to make enough space on the web server, and since the deposition was hard copy and not electronically available as a download, some manual labor was going to be involved to scan each and every page by hand.

I won't bore you with the specific posts revealing their intentions. What I will do is share Clark's written musings:

> "I think all of this information along with the court records I have should be sent to all of the media. What do you think (Smith)? I think if the media knew who has been behind a lot of the chain yanking they would have a better understanding of what is going on."

The media? She wants to send my deposition *to the media?* I have highly sensitive information about the parents I've worked with and their children in there—each of their names protected by a court order—and now she wants to expose these innocent people and their personal pain to any and all takers? In my testimony there were even details regarding my dealings with a celebrity who had a son in a program. Fodder for the tabloids perhaps?

That Clark and company apparently had no hesitation in exposing these families to get back at me was . . . shocking, appalling. And what about *my* family? Even my daughter's confidential medical information was a subject of discussion in this deposition, and to think the world at large would be privy to such intimate details about my child made my blood boil.

Go after me, and that's one thing. Go after my child, and get ready to take me on. Having my Social Security number publicly posted so I could deal with all kinds of potential identity theft paled in comparison to my daughter, my son—and all those sons and daughters belonging to someone else—being subjected to the scrutiny of a mass audience composed of the curious, the happenstance viewer, parents, professionals, and no telling who else, with no doubt a few perverts thrown in.

With this single threat the gloves came off. To put it mildly, the famous line from the movie *Network* says it all: *I'm mad as hell, and I'm not going to take it anymore!*

I have no idea what kind of chain yanking Clark was referring to, but she crossed a line by involving the children, and that's a place that she never should have gone.

Finally, *finally*, goaded into action—it was just a few days before Christmas—I got busy and fast. I notified my Utah attorney, who immediately served a cease-and-desist letter as well as a motion for a preliminary injunction and a motion to seal court records. As the judge began to understand what was happening to me, he issued these rulings in his order:

"The court has made clear to counsel that its primary concern was the prevention of the public disclosure of the names of children who have been placed in the various programs subject to this litigation. The names of children are *not* to be disclosed in public court proceedings.

No other information about Ms. Scheff shall be disclosed in public pleadings.

The parties may not disclose outside of this litigation confidential financial information or confidential trade secrets learned during discovery.

To minimize the risk of improper disclosure of information, all future depositions in this case shall be attorneys only. Any depositions taken before this order may only be used by the attorneys and their clients only. Any depositions posted on websites or made available to the public must be removed."

Thank you, Judge Cassell.

Although my attorney's letter and motion put Clark and Smith on notice even before the judge could issue his order, enough rumblings of disgruntlement on the website let me know that I might have won this battle but they had no intentions of losing the war on me and PURE.

Since PURE is based in Florida, my wonderful attorney in Utah advised me to get representation in my home state. I still had some supporters and professional colleagues who had remained loyal that I could call on for advice. One of them gave me the name of a lawyer who didn't specialize in Internet law (I didn't even know there was such a thing), but I was told he was damn good.

I had the number. It was the day before Christmas Eve, 2003, and my hands were still shaking from equal measures of rage and desperation as I hit the keypad. A pleasant voice answered. "Law offices of David Pollack, may I help you?"

"Yes. My name is Sue Scheff. I need to speak to Mr. Pollack immediately."

Information Yearns to Be Free

Protecting Evidence in Litigation

It's a sign of the times. While our legal system has rules preventing the destruction or spoiling (spoliation) of evidence, as well as rules that under certain circumstances can prevent the public disclosure of information through a court's decision to close a file to the public ("sealing" of the case), we have yet to effectively implement rules that protect evidence from public distribution absent exceptional circumstances. The reticence of the courts to limit the free flow of information and access to public trials is grounded in our Constitution. But in this new day and age, the damage done by publicizing certain evidence can outweigh the harm caused by misconduct that brought about the lawsuit in the first place. There is a struggle, by now a common one, between the "information yearns to be free" crowd and everyone else who values their right to privacy. Yes, it is a continuing theme.

You must understand what can become public in a lawsuit if you are considering legal action. Otherwise, embarrassing or damaging information can make it into the public arena much more easily today than in the past, thanks to the Internet. And the likelihood of it getting online is much greater today since your adversaries often understand the harm they can inflict on you. As a general rule, almost no private information is off-limits in discovery, which is the phase in which both sides discover the evidence of the case by using written inquiries, obtaining documents, and asking questions in depositions. How, then, do we protect private information when it cannot be controlled? Courts are hesitant to "seal" a file completely. I've been involved in fewer than six cases in which the entire case was sealed. Assume your case will not be sealed, and even if it is at the time of filing, expect it to be unsealed quickly as the case moves forward.

But the court can issue "protective orders" requiring that the public not have access to certain information. Usually this is worked out in advance by the lawyers with a detailed multitiered protective order. Sue would have been much better off addressing this issue earlier in the litigation. The failure to do so is one big reason why she finds herself faced with the threat that very private information about her, her family, her clients, and others will be published on the web for all to see in perpetuity. Note that the judge ordered everything already posted on the web to be removed. Does anyone think that can really effectively happen? No. There is little chance of truly taking back information that finds its way online. So the issue needs to be addressed proactively up front when in litigation. This means that in particularly sensitive legal cases, requests can be made to the judge to seal all, or part, of a case to avoid public disclosure. But before any information is exchanged with the other side, either through initial disclosures mandated by court rules to start the case off or the beginning of the discovery phase, your lawyer must evaluate what subjects and evidence and information should be protected and propose the entry of a "protective order" that will limit distribution appropriately to only those who need to know and are involved in the case.

What kind of information can come out in a deposition? Everything. Your medical condition, your Social Security number, the amount of your bank balances, and on and on. Depositions are a veritable treasure trove for identity thieves and those who wish to do harm to your reputation and get you sued by others. Think about it. In the past, secrets and confidences would be leaked to friends or maybe the local newspaper. But today your bank account and Social Security numbers can end up on a foreign website used as a haven and clearinghouse by thieves. The passwords you had to give up in the deposition can be placed on a hacker community website. Your photo, age, marital status, and address can be shared with sexual predators on forums. All of this in seconds. So, the laws must change, the judges must appreciate the risks involved, and the lawyers need to be much more careful when litigating cases in court.

That's another strong reason why our privacy laws need to be re-energized. I'll be discussing that shortly. Funny how the courts insist upon maintaining "access to the courts" and resist protecting private information with no apparent appreciation for the fact that many people avoid accessing the courts out of fear of losing their privacy.

Information yearns to be free? Congress doesn't think so. There is the Health Insurance Portability and Accountability Act of 1996 (HIPAA) to protect medical records and the Fair Credit Reporting Act to protect financial information, and all kinds of information and data protection laws on the books and in the works. Let's apply just a little bit of that level of concern to protecting some of the most damaging information that is presented as evidence in cases.

If You Are Going to San Francisco

Privacy Laws

Let's go back in time. In 1888, Eastman patented the Kodak roll-film camera. In 1890, a *Harvard Law Review* article called for the establishment and legal protection of individual rights to privacy. Coincidence? I think not. Laws evolve in relation to historical trends and events. At least they used to. In 1890, it seemed that the traditional notions of the right to be left alone were at risk by the advance of technology. Over the following sixty years the right to privacy grew right alongside the new media invasion: first the moving motion picture, then talkies, followed by radio and television. But by the 1960s, a funny thing was happening. The counterculture revolution was beginning to emerge. Free love, free drugs, and free speech were becoming the bedrock of a new generation. Individual privacy rights began to give way in popularity to the concept of free everything, including the expansion of free speech.

By the 1990s, the intrusion of solitude laws protecting against unwanted invasions of one's private quarters were in disfavor. The laws against the public disclosure of truthful, but private, facts were under attack. Protections against the publication of true facts that place a person in a false light were waning. Only commercial appropriation claims seemed to remain viable. These changes were a result of a famous law professor who wrote that privacy protections were no longer needed.

We are now fifteen years into the commercialization of the Internet. And it's hard to see any movement yet toward greater protections of individual privacy. This is surprising when one compares the personal intrusions of the camera to the personal intrusions visited upon each of us by the Web. It's hard to say why law professors aren't more vocal in calling for greater privacy protections. One theory holds that the professors are too worried about being attacked online to speak their mind. I have to concede that the free-speechers out there have a long and nasty history of attacking the speech of those with whom they disagree. Being held up on the web to scorn, ridicule, satire, sarcasm, and vicious defamatory attacks is probably not the road to tenure, and is certainly not appealing to the profs who have to go in and face their constituents each morning in class.

The foundation of the web was built on the concept of a free and open environment, and since commercialization of the Internet took off in the San Francisco area (forever identified by Haight-Ashbury, the "summer of love," and flowers in your hair), it makes sense that the foundations and norms and mores of the web evolved around a commitment to free speech—a concept that has been passed down through the generations. Privacy rights never had a chance in this new medium.

But change is coming. You see, one of my favorite cities is San Francisco. It's the Key West and Provincetown of the West Coast times ten. Open minds are everywhere in the San Fran area. And I wouldn't be surprised if it leads the way in reforming privacy laws so that balanced protections of personal rights and public participation and free speech can coexist. When that happens, the rest of the nation will follow.

MONKEYS DON'T FLY

"Cast wishful thinking and false assumptions aside. Even the Scarecrow was smart enough to fight."

I wish I had been clever enough to think that up but John gets all the credit. It's something he told me recently when we were discussing at what point I had been pushed so far into a corner that I had no choice but to fight back.

The last week of December in 2003 is one I'll never forget, and no amount of wishful thinking can change the unfolding events that would soon come to change my life in some profound and disturbing ways.

The "complaint and demand for jury trial" was filed against Clark on December 31st. The same day I learned about the Broward County PTA posting. Guess we both had a Happy New Year's Eve. To the PTA's credit, as soon as I alerted them to the situation, they immediately removed the post.

While my attorney David Pollack moved aggressively forward, I vacated my office. Something had to go with the cost of litigating this case, and the office outside my home was a casualty of that expense. Not that it was all that hard to give up since I was having increasing difficulty dealing with the emotional repercussions, and home felt like a safe haven where I wouldn't have to show my face in public.

Over the next two and a half years, there was a lot to hide my face in embarrassment about. Enough that I was never able to bring myself to share any of this with my parents, siblings, or anyone else who wasn't directly involved with the whole sordid affair.

How sordid? There came a point that if you did a Google search on "Sue Scheff," one of the top three results had a link to "Sue Scheff's Red Panties." And if you clicked onto the link, just guess where it took the viewer? You got it: Smith's website.

Due to the graphic nature of the following posts, those with more delicate sensibilities are advised to skip to the next page.

> **From Anonymous:** "Susan, I would endure [redacted] to be able to put my face in your pu**y for 10 minutes, especially if you were wearing some red panties!"
>
> **Anonymous #2 responds:** "I want to hear about her panties, damn it!!"
>
> **Anonymous #3 chimes in:** "Susan, I will mail you $50 for a pair of red panties worn by YOU and UNWASHED. PLEASE don't deny me this pleasure. . . ."
>
> **Anonymous #4:** "Susan Scheff's red panties must be made of silky-smooth SATIN and smell LOVELY after she wears them all day!"
>
> **Anonymous #5:** "Susan, I'm thinking LONG and HARD about this before I say it: I'll bet my left testicle that you are wearing RED PANTIES RIGHT NOW!!!!"

Anonymous #6: "Oh, it works for ME!! Oooooooohhhhhh, yeeeeaah-hhh!!!! GodDAMN I'm gonna have to go for about 15 minutes . . . that oughta do it. . . . bb ltr. . . ."

And this was in the top three results of a Google search for my name.

Can anyone, *anyone,* tell me when it became permissible in our society to spew pornographic vomit all over a woman—or a man for that matter—while hiding behind the veil of anonymity and the perverse twisting of our precious First Amendment rights?

I think the depravity of these posts speak for themselves. Four days after the original postings, Smith responded with this abbreviated posting of her own:

"Ok, folks. In case anyone is wondering what happened to the red panties posts, here's the story.

Sue was not at all amused w/those posts…However, it really isn't up to me to decide what is and is not proper conduct or legitimate communication around here. But I have good reason to believe that she was so upset by this that she was willing to litigate. So then I figured out who was posting those messages and asked whether or not (he/they) wanted me to delete them. (He/they) did, and so they're gone. . . .

For future reference, let me reiterate and clarify my policy on controlling the content here. I try not to put myself in the middle if at all possible, except by way of participation in public discussion. Of course I'm responsible for what I write.

If it's an anon post and the author wants it changed or deleted, I'll do that. Done it many times. But it really is up to the author whether or not the content in question is worth fighting for."

Really? Does that mean the posts would remain on Smith's website
to this day if the anon poster(s) she was able to trace had decided
their sexually graphic musings specifically targeted at me were worth
fighting for? And since they were gracious enough to delete their
naughty bits of fun, I suppose I'm expected to pretend it never happened in the first place, any feelings of violation gone as quick as the
"click" of a mouse.

"There's no place like home. . . . " Click, click. *"There's no place like
home. . . . "*

Click. Click. With each "click" of a computer mouse to search for
my name on Google, complete paranoia claimed squatter's rights in
my soul and in my psyche. The accumulated damage went deep.
"There's no place like home. . . . " Home was a safe house I took refuge in
and increasingly did not want to leave. As long as I stayed away from
the Internet search engines, I was safe within the cosseting walls of my
home. The same residence I had to mortgage in order to keep fighting for what little was left of the tattered reputation attached to my
name—a name that came to serve up over *two pages* of initial Google
results, in the form of topic headings that linked directly to Smith's
website.

And how could something like this happen, you might wonder?
The posters had created forum after forum after forum with such
enticing eye-catchers as "Sue Scheff Lies" and "PURE Bullshit."

And what about PURE over the course of nearly three years in
cyberhell? My beautiful baby took a real beating but managed to limp
along despite what had ballooned into a classic case of agoraphobia.
When I made myself leave the house, I would no longer make eye contact with anyone at the grocery store. I still had to eat, even though I
had little appetite, and between my weight loss and inability to sleep,

I could hardly recognize myself in the mirror. Go to a restaurant and meet some friends for dinner or happy hour? I had become so reclusive that most of my friends no longer bothered to ask, and since even ordering a latte at Starbucks was a challenge, a larger venue was out of the question. I didn't want to meet anyone new for fear they would ask me my name or want to know where I worked, then decide to do a casual Google search just out of curiosity.

Despite all the trash piled on top of my name and PURE's website, some families in need still managed to find us. Fortunately I had an associate who would return phone calls because I had shut down to the point that I had difficulty speaking to family members, and that included my own. As for the personal meetings I had once so loved to have with parents, those were a thing of the past. So were speaking engagements, community workshops, interfacing with school counselors—anything that involved outside verbal or physical contact required more internal stamina than I was able to summon.

I had always been an outgoing people person and never imagined I could be reduced to such a shell of my former self. I knew I needed some kind of therapy to work through this awful situation that was eating me alive. And while I did speak privately with my educational psychologist colleague, who would later testify on my behalf, I could not bring myself to act on his advice to seek the necessary help that I desperately needed. Why? Because I was afraid that somehow a visit to a psychologist or psychiatrist would leak out and become public knowledge on the Internet. I know how ridiculous that must sound, but my paranoia had reached a point that I felt like Dorothy without Kansas or Oz in sight, only flying wild monkeys swooping down and landing all around me, screeching and tearing at my hair, any which way I turned.

And weren't they? After all, even if I managed to escape the paranoia and agoraphobia, I could slide straight into *schizophrenia* since I
had apparently adopted an evil twin who had assumed my identity
online.

"There's no place like home. . . . " Click, click. *"There's no place like home. . . ."*

Home, unfortunately, offered no protection from my alter ego who
appeared as a "guest" on a far too familiar website, and, in suitably
large letters, posted this request:

"My dearest (Smith),

I do not understand. I have asked you for my very own message
peg board on your website but you do not respond to my pleas. I had
to make my request on the [redacted] forum. Humiliating! Why won't
you have a forum for:

PURE and ME, Sue Scheff?

Why Smith? I beg you. Why all others but none for ME?

I'm wondering if maybe you could start a forum all about me, yes
ME, ME AND ME, and more ME. Oh, and please include my bestest
friend [redacted].

I wove woo, Smith.

—Sue Scheff

P.S. Oh yeah, please include my PURE as a dove sign because I'm
PURE and innocent in RED!"

An open call was then extended to the completely open-to-the-
public forum:

LET'S TAKE A VOTE FOR A FORUM FOR ONLY SUE SCHEFF AND
PURE AS A DOVE. . . .

And as expected, this was a very popular idea. Per one respondent:

> "I vote 'yes' for a dedicated forum for Sue Scheff and PURE. Good idea. Why not? She is asking and I say go for it. Great idea, Sue!"

The "bestest friend" whose name I redacted was also singled out for a cyberlynching because of her association with me. I won't heap more potential spitting upon her than she's already endured by publicly exposing her identity.

As for my plea being granted for a personal bulletin board and forum dedicated to ME, ME, and ME, the generosity of the givers allowed me to also speak for "myself" in the general forum—although that schizophrenia thing kept cropping up since I went from posting as "Sue Scheff," to "Lawsuit Sue," to "Not Sue Scheff" (please note, even "Not Sue Scheff" responded on the forum as if she were, indeed, still me).

Let's see . . . so many posts in my various names on this forum, it's really hard to pick just one since my username information on the site reveals "I" was posting an average of 11.98 messages per day. Okay, eeny, meeny, miny, moe! Here's a couple that'll do for giggles and grins:

> **From Anonymous:** "SUE, SUE, SUE . . . what programs do you refer to and what is the criteria they have to meet to be deemed worthy of PURE?"
>
> **From Lawsuit Sue, A regular around here:** "If you people continue to misrepresent my business practices, I hope you are prepared for expensive and unpleasant litigation. I am one of the good people in all of this. IT IS VERY IMPORTANT THAT ALL YOU REMEMBER THAT! And once again, thank you for your interest in PURE."

From Anonymous: "Sue, you are not one of the good ones ... you are one of the bad ones in my opinion. Stupid bitch."

From Not Susan Scheff, familiar face: "I believe I explained in one of my prior posts what I mean by reasonable precautions. If you did not understand then . . . GIVE ME A BREAK! It is obvious that your brain operates at a slower pace than a turtle moves around! I am one of the good people in all of this." (Posted from Florida)

After this had gone on awhile and "I" had assumed several Sue Scheff identities, Smith intervened with this Pontius Pilate hands-off "warning":

"In case there was any doubt at all, I changed the name of user 'Susan Scheff' to 'NOT Susan Scheff' pending contact with the prankster who's been writing under that name. I did think it was funny as hell there for a while, but I had no idea that anyone would actually believe that it was really Susan Scheff writing that stuff! Satire, folks, satire!

Now, as to some of the other content here regarding Susan: I stand by my terms of use and usual policy. I'm not responsible, legally or ethically, for what you folks decide to write. And I'm in no hurry to assist anyone who may get bent out of shape over it. But, now this is important, I can be legally compelled to cooperate w/discovery if some litigious person decides they want to sue you for it!"

So yet again, Smith has washed her hands as website administrator while high-fiving "the prankster" and turning a blind eye to yet another "prank" in full view of anyone visiting her website: an e-mail address "I" was making available along with "my" posts. Seems one of my alter egos decided to set up an e-mail account in the name of Sue

Scheff and respond in my name to whoever "would actually believe that it was really Susan Scheff."

As John so eloquently put it, *"Cast wishful thinking and false assumptions aside. Even the Scarecrow was smart enough to fight."*

But that didn't stop me from wishful thinking. If only I knew what I ever did to incur Clark's wrath, which spread like a cancer to eager followers who had never met me and really knew nothing about me at all. If only I could make the last three years disappear as if they had never happened. If only I had more than a Calgon bath to take me away. Like maybe a pair of ruby slippers?

"There's no place like home. . . ." Click, click. *"There's no place like home. . . ."*

The Best Defense Is Offense?

Lawsuit Considerations

Every situation is different. Sue chose a lawsuit as the centerpiece of her counterattack. In football games we hear the commentators point out that the best defense is a strong offense. But throwing deep passes is the most aggressive counterattack and how many interceptions and quarterback sacks do we see when an attack not only goes airborne, but deep? A lot. High risk. High reward. Dealing with online attacks is no different.

A lawsuit carries with it serious risks. The initial publicity could spur on a "mobosphere" attack by those who take offense to anyone putting in play the notion that "information yearns to be free." There could be attempts to smother the plaintiff into submission by swarming together and attacking like African honey bees. A high profile "consumer-rights" group could jump in to offer a free legal defense to the attacker, and, at the same time, intentionally motivate its constituents to undertake attacks. It's a common occurrence. You, and your family, could be placed in a position of compromise with false attacks emanating from the hinterlands all over the world. Your lawyer could be targeted, and his reputation and his law firm's reputation could be attacked. I've seen many a lawyer, shell-shocked from an initial wave of negative commentary and false attacks, run from a case as quickly as he can. Now you are out in the cold, and a lot worse off.

So, what Sue did took courage. And I've just painted for you the reason why there is a paucity of lawsuits over online defamation. One reason, as we've seen, is the "Streisand Effect." Interesting, isn't it, that those believing so firmly in free speech and the concept of information flowing without bounds are so ready to attack the speech of those who object? The netizens of the mobosphere, their supporters and their followers, are all for free speech. Until, of course, they don't agree with it. And trust me when I tell you that they don't like any of their compatriots to be sued, no matter the egregious nature of the misconduct.

But a lawsuit isn't the only way to aggressively and openly fight back. Inventors, for instance, seem to often be at the center of online disputes. Once in a while, a valuable innovation comes along and an inventor reaps great financial rewards, but more often than not the inventor's only reward is the gratitude of, and attribution from, others. Steal an invention from an inventor, claim it as your own, and you are asking for trouble.

So it was when an inventor asked me for help. An online businessman was using his "baby" and claiming it as his own. There was a lot of intellectual capital tied up in the inventor's work, and he was naturally upset. And thus we see another form of counterattack, one of the most successful I have ever witnessed. This scofflaw didn't know the first thing about reputation management. He had left himself exposed. He was regaling in a spike in business, but wearing a birthday suit fit for a king, if you get my drift. He had left himself naked. The first page results on Google weren't under his control. This is a prime example of how the effect of not proactively managing your online reputation comes into play. Results that Google considered to be of importance and highly authoritative when this individual's name was searched did not exist. So it wasn't hard to jump over the results populating prime organic or natural search positions (search results generated by Google's algorithm and not "sponsored" or paid results). This was an invitation for intervention through counterinsurgency. The lesson you can learn is that if you don't build up your own online reputation by using my recommended techniques, you are asking for trouble, and when it comes knocking you'll have no defense except an open door with a welcome mat.

Mr. Inventor spent a couple of hours videotaping messages, very credible and sincere ones at that, explaining that this company had stolen his invention. He then posted the videos and used some optimization techniques on YouTube targeting the thieving company's name. The next day, both videos were on the first page of Google results. Needless to say, the begging began immediately, and didn't end until the true inventor had a nice licensing deal in place. He took the snap, avoided a blitzing linebacker, rolled out to his right, and threw a bomb across his body to the tight end streaking down the left hash mark for a ninety-nine-yard touchdown! Sweet.

Another masterful counterpunch came from a surgeon. He was a doctor's doctor. You know, the kind of doc that other doctors go to. It's the highest compliment, and he was in high regard all over the world. Not a blemish on his record; pretty remarkable given the highly emotional nature of his type of surgery patients. Let's set the stage: As retirement approaches, one naturally starts to think about your legacy. What will I be remembered for? Will my children, and their children, be proud of my contributions to society? And so it goes. As the day nears for retirement the phone rings at the office. And it's the nightmare of all nightmares. The voice on the other line explains that a television network is doing an exposé on surgeon butchers and they would like to include him for a "botched" surgery on a former patient. Immediately he envisions his spotless career record being overwhelmed by the online commentary and follow-on false attacks that are sure to follow such an exposé.

We were brought onto the crisis management team immediately. Of course, he couldn't comment on the allegations because of federal laws prohibiting the release of a patient's records without written permission. His response was quick and to the point. "I can't comment or even consider participation on your program because I don't have a medical records release." Within days he obtained a full medical records release. Our surgeon client then launched a website detailing the exact treatment provided, vividly illustrating the work performed, pointing out the inaccuracies in the photographs provided by this former patient, and laying out in great detail his expertise, reputation, and the case for why the surgery performed achieved a stellar result. The last I heard, the seemingly credible TV guest was discredited and uninvited. And the surgeon's problem was over. Sometimes you can play aggressive offense by running that big fullback right up the gut of the defense. Make sure you control the line of scrimmage first, though.

Aggressive responses are high risk. We don't live in a world of "my lawyer will deal with it." At least not anymore. It is far too complex an environment to view a demand letter, a cease and desist, a lawsuit, or any other type of legal communication as the immediate solution. For lawyers, the days of firing off a preformatted letter are a thing of the past. If you assert a legal claim in such a letter and threaten legal action, the recipient can sue you for a "declaratory judgment" in his home town in an effort to outmaneuver you. You become a defendant rather than a plaintiff in a far off place with expensive, new lawyers. Or the letter will be posted online and generate publicity that encourages even more problems. Or the law firm will be attacked. And judging from the very weak search engine optimization techniques employed by most law firms, even rudimentary mobosphere attacks can have an immediate and lasting effect. So make sure when you are under attack you get the right players involved. You can figure out which lawyers and consultants have solid expertise in the specific field of online defamation, and I'll tell you what to look for. But for now, remember that quarterbacks with weak offensive lines get concussions.

The Wild West Show

Google Bomb

Concussions in the online world come from Google Bombs. "Google Bomb" refers to anchored text linking practices intended to influence the ranking of particular pages in results returned by the Google search engine. An anchored text link looks like any other link that you click on in order to go to the web content described. A normal anchor text link actually describes the destination of the link. So you can decide in advance whether you want to visit the linked-to content by the description.

But an anchored text link used in a Google Bomb has an entirely different effect. The link generally does not accurately describe the content to which the link points. So, if a group of people want to use a Google Bomb to attack you, they will point anchored text links to their websites or blogs or social network profiles with your name as the words that are in the link. But the page linked to actually contains derogatory or defamatory content. Then along comes Google's spiders; they associate the defamatory content page as being you, based on the description in the links, and when someone searches for you, Google presents it as a result. At the same time, the misleading links from others to the defamatory page are seen by Google as a vote for the authority of the page, so the site is given a hyperboost in importance and prominence by Google in search results. It's a double whammy. Because of the coming together of these two effects through the use of a Google Bomb, the defamatory site will show up whenever your name is searched, often at the top of the results depending upon the scope of the Google Bomb.

Here is the computer code of an anchor text link: *<a href="http://dozier-internet-law.blogspot.com/">***Dozier Internet Law on Trademark**</a> The italicized words (for emphasis) designate the web property the link will lead to. The bold words (again for emphasis) are supposed to describe the content located at the site linked to. In this instance, you would see a link on the page that reads "Dozier Internet Law on Trademark," and by clicking on it you would go to our law firm blog on trademark law. This is the way anchored text links are supposed to work.

Now, here is the computer code of an anchor text link in a Google Bomb: *<a href="http://www.XYZsucks.com/">***Your Name Here**</a>. Notice that the link will show as your name on the page, but will actually lead to a site that attacks you. That's the foundation of a Google Bomb, and this tactic is used in just about every online attack to position negative and derogatory and defamatory lies on the first page of Google results when the target name is searched.

So, the URL to which the link points is buried in the HTML code of the webpage, and not visible to the reader. The only thing a visitor sees is the description of the link, placed there not to accurately describe the content to which the link points, but to mislead Google. The link description Google needs to return accurate and reliable search results has been hijacked.

That's in great part what is happening to Sue. Really offensive and profane comments begin showing up as the third result when she is searched in Google. Soon the first two pages are dominated as more and more web properties of all sorts are launched and Sue's name is repeated time and again. Cross-linking between the posts and comments and content falsely lead Google to treat those pages as belonging to Sue Scheff. So they are presented as organic results when she and PURE are searched. With an impact only Sue can really explain.

All of this is possible because Google relies heavily upon democratization concepts and has built its processes to give heavy weight to the "virtual vote" of netizens (citizens of the web). Google's robots go out onto the web and when they run across an anchored text link they make a note of this fact. Then when the search result algorithms are implemented, Google uses the anchor text link description for independent verification of the contents of a page. After all, the anchored text descriptions should be very reliable since third parties are describing the content, and results are intended to deliver the most relevant result. The link also adds authority to the page since by this link Google concludes that the public is saying "this is important." And while Google has tried to fix this problem in the more notorious cases, the fact remains that Google fundamentally believes in empowering the masses and presenting results by popular vote of the online citizenry. So it's hard to see how this problem will be remedied any time soon. And the concept that links provide valid, independent insight and credible guidance as to the value and importance and authoritative reputation of a webpage makes a lot of sense. So the solution is a tough one for Google to figure out.

The most notorious Google Bomb ever was the "mass link prank" visited upon President Bush. If you looked up "miserable failure" his White House webpage was the first result, and President Obama inherited it for a while when he took office. But all Google Bombs are not so prominent or notorious. In fact, most Google Bombs are not even recognized as such because the mechanism that detonates the Google Bomb is a common utilitarian device (anchored text link) put to use for good and bad everyday, and many times over. Up to now, if an attack was well known, it was a Google Bomb. If not well known, no one noticed. We all need to take more notice of this problem and work toward finding a solution.

That's how a Google Bomb works.

Now let's consider how else you can get Google Bombed.

1. A competitor launches a page or a site and a huge volume of links to that site from its own pages or from pages spread all over the world (that's really easy to do) with your business name as the anchor text. Its site starts showing up in results when people try to locate you.

2. An affiliate marketer selling a competing product or service acquires a high number of anchored text links in your name and points them all to a page that may not even have any competing content on it . . . yet. But once it gets a prime ranking, watch out.

3. A group of bloggers and commentators run across a particularly false and unflattering article about you, your kids, or your business. Each individual posts his own snarky and biting comments, restating and rehashing the lies, with a liberal sprinkling (usually three for optimal effect) of anchored text links pointing to the defamatory article. And then every blogger feeds off of one another by linking back to the criticisms voiced by each other. All of the links are anchored with your name. Now you have a massive problem with many, many pages dominating search results when someone looks for you.

Number three is known as a "blog swarm" or a "mobosphere attack." Of course mob justice is an oxymoron. These are coordinated yet highly decentralized attacks perpetrated by unconventional and unlawful means. And we are seeing the effects of such an attack on Sue. She is undergoing an e-lynching. And while there are many other tricks for the mobosphere to use, the ability to Google Bomb is the powerful instigator and progenitor. The mobosphere's Google Bomb is the town crier, the witness, the judge, the jury, and the executioner all rolled up in one. And the bloggers, social networkers, social bookmarkers, forum posters, website owners, and the like all grab their torches and join the march to the jail. It's as if you can hear them muttering, "he's in jail and he's been charged . . . he must be guilty."

When you hear me talk in terms of the web being in a Wild West stage of lawlessness, that's what I mean. As Sue is quickly learning.

Anatomy of a Google Bomb and Mobosphere Attack

Google Bomb Revisited

Sue is being hit from all sides, and the instigator and lead attacker appear to have some followers, but not so many that they can step back and have others act as a proxy and do the dirty work for them. The Google Bomber you really have to be on the lookout for is a leader, an authority figure, of a web constituency. As I write this in February 2009, I am watching a Google Bomb attack developing with the leadership of the Public Citizen Litigation Group and Paul Alan Levy. Public Citizen claims to have over 100,000 members, so that is quite an influential constituency to energize. You would think lawyers, particularly ones actually appearing in cases, would never consider instigating an online mob attack against a party to the case. But that is exactly what Levy is doing. And he appears to his constituents, mostly free-speech expansionsists and web-democratization fanatics, as a real leader and an authority figure.

After all, they reason: he seems to always give us the advice we want to hear! I am reminded of the guidance I received in law school from a prominent and controversial federal district judge about positioning arguments before judges. "Pound the facts when the facts are in your favor, pound the law when the law is in your favor, and when neither is in your favor, pound the table." Levy is pounding the table. Of necessity. I view him and his legal team at Public Citizen as the primary protectors for the gross misconduct of scofflaws online. In the mobosphere he is the Godfather. Here's a good example:

It's Friday, February 20, 2009 at 5:38 PM. A preferred time to launch an attack on a business. The technology staff has left for the weekend. Word is out that

Jones Day, the 2,000-lawyer law firm, has just settled a lawsuit by forcing a small Internet company to stop "anchor text" linking to its website. And Paul Alan Levy, having filed a brief in the case as a "friend of the court" supporting the small company, but still smarting from the judge's refusal to even consider his arguments, is obviously not happy. His blog post doesn't just include ranting about unethical lawyers and judges. It's not apparent whether the typical mass e-mail went out with his rant to Public Citizen's 100,000 members, but the next day, all hell breaks loose. First, we'll look at what happened, and then analyze what Levy did to incite a Google Bomb and mobosphere attack.

On Slashdot.com the day after Levy's post:

"I wonder if the owners of jonesdaysucks.com feel the same way."

"I get the feeling that they are soon to learn about what is called the Streisand Effect."

"At least you didn't link to gay porn, or child porn, or beastiality, or golden showers, or shit-eaters. . . . "(all anchored text links pointing to the Jones Day website).

"We are going about this the wrong way . . . Jones Day, Jones Day, Jones Day (Don't click on the links, trust me) . . . maybe we can get Jones Day the law firm off the front page of Google." (all anchored text links apparently pointing to dangerous sites for your computer).

"I have a feeling Jones Day, are about to have a really bad day."

"Hello? Streisand Effect?"

"The whole Google-Bomb idea was nice. . . . "

" . . . the judge in the case refused to even look at the brief. . . . "

"Yes, Judge Darrah, I just said you're either incompetent or crooked."

"Or you can rate him here. This should get interesting. . . . "

Within forty-eight hours, the website that offers a rating system on judges (The Robing Room) is inundated with over 100 ratings, many from "lawyers." Prior to February 22, the judge had received a total of seven reviews in almost three years. Overnight he has become a very popular subject:

"the judge in this case refused to even look at the brief."

"poor temperment, probably crooked."

"What a disgrace to the legal system."

"What a total f*cktard asshole c*ck-knocker. He once tried to fondle my kid brother and offered me oral sex in the bathroom of his courthouse."

"Refusing to look at a brief because the opposing side says it is biased is unconsionable (sic)."

"Biased, lazy, arrogant."

"A disgrace to the system."

"In addition to corrupt, throw in incompetent."

"Corrupt Judge."

"he is an incompetent and corrupt baffoon (sic)."

"biased, degenerative."

"A judge should look at every brief submitted to him."

"Terrible, terrible judge."

"You're a f*cking disgrace."

"Crooked, corrupt, incompetent."

"This rating system is broken . . . a 1 is too generous."

"Complete Yankee dickhead."

"Try actually viewing briefs put before you, Judge."

So, we have a little bit of everything here. Google Bombing, the Streisand Effect, and a sucks site. The "don't click on the links" reference is to try to get these linked pages showing up as Jones Day search results so when people click on them their computer could be hijacked or a virus downloaded. Other sites discuss e-mailing the law firm and just about every variation of a Google Bomb and mobosphere attack we discuss.

Now, what exactly did Levy do to instigate this kind of madness? He attacked the judge in the case. "The very fact that the trial judge allowed this case to drag on, rather than dismissing it outright based on the sound reasons that Public Citizen and the Electronic Frontier Foundation (EFF) put forward in our amicus brief. . ." is an outrage according to Levy, continuing his theme first voiced when he claimed the judge refused to listen to him. What comes next is worse, though. He repeated "Jones Day" as an anchored text link twenty-nine times in his blog post. Some of these were links to derogatory articles or to a photograph on the Public Citizen website of the asses of two horses. If there is any doubt about his intentions, read his own words:

"One might, however, suggest that the Internet community to [sic] fight back against Jones Day, by repeatedly deep-linking from its name, and to its website, in precisely the ways to which it objects, but which it cannot prevent through litigation. Jones Day's bullies should learn that they cannot have their way. In addition to linking to Jones Day's own website, the community can use hyperlinks to show Jones

Day what they think of its abuse of free speech online. Does Jones Day really believe in its theories of the case? Let's find out. In the end, Jones Day will have to accept the limits of its bullying power."

That is a call to his Internet constituency to fight back with a Google Bomb. And his attacks on the judge had the intended effect of inciting a virtual riot and mob attack on the judge's reputation. Evolving quickly from Levy's request to attack were a panoply of mobosphere attacks from all directions.

My Weapon of Choice Is E-mail

E-mail Abuse

The attacks Levy has precipitated also involve e-mail. The attackers discuss some tactics in general terms and coy suggestions. Sue is also battling the problem of people opening e-mail accounts using her name and sending who knows what out to others. I've had the same problem. E-mail as a weapon is very dangerous.

Imagine you are always the first one in the office every morning. You got it from your father, who got it from his father, the founder of your 100-year-old small-town business. Most powerful retailers stay in business an average of fifty years, so there is a certain comfort in knowing that you'll be handing a well-respected, well-oiled, and reasonably profitable store over to your eldest son when he returns from college graduation this year.

As you open the door, you have a sense that something is amiss. As you walk through the office, you notice message lights for all the phones blinking. Immediately you panic, thinking that a loved one has been trying to reach someone . . . anyone . . . to get some help. You quickly grab the receiver with your left hand, hit your message key with your right index finger, and find out your voicemail is full. For the next twenty minutes, you listen to one threatening message after another from people all over the country. Some are coming to visit, one with a gun. Others are going to sue, or have contacted the Federal Bureau of Investigation and the Federal Trade Commission and the state attorney general. As you look up, you are happy to see a friendly face. Your local sheriff is pulling into the parking lot to check up on things. He's been getting a lot of very weird telephone calls about you.

Your business is under attack. As you slept, an employee you fired last week was sending millions upon millions of spam e-mails out "advertising" your store. And worst of all, the e-mails were asking the outraged recipients to call. The unspeakable content of the e-mails, coupled with obvious violations of the federal CAN-SPAM Act (the federal law regulating the use of commercial e-mail), was quite adequate motivation for people from all over North America to do just that. As the day progresses, your employees are all getting chewed out, ultimately saved from their misery only by the silence caused when your telephone system is overwhelmed. Your e-mail server has long ago stopped functioning, clogged up with a veritable deluge of incoming e-mails. And your website has gone offline also, as if someone had orchestrated a "denial of service" attack. In the coming days, you will start noticing the vicious online attacks about your business. And you will soon find out that your small store has been reported to an Australian spam tracking company that then downloads the IP addresses of spammers to its subscriber base of ISPs all over the world. As you send e-mails, the ISPs are filtering them out as spam without notice. And the internal reporting systems at AOL and Microsoft have already placed your e-mail address domain and IP address on "blacklists," effectively intercepting many e-mails you send out.

Am I making this up? Wish I was. Several days went by before I got the call and was hired. Even though it has been several years, I still remember the pain and panic in our client's voice on that first call. The biggest concern at that moment was the thought of another round of e-mails. Everyone in the office was scared. And, by the way, business was at a standstill. We immediately communicated directly with the prime suspect. I explained that we did not know who was doing this, but that we would find out, and if it was him he was likely going to learn about the realities of life in a very stark, harsh way.

No other attacks were forthcoming. And as we assessed the situation it became apparent that the FBI couldn't help us. They would only pay attention to a federal violation of CAN-SPAM if at least $100,000 was stolen. Our client, reflecting the class and good judgment obviously at the heart of the century-old business success story, knew the kid had nothing from which to recover a civil judgment. "Let's cut our losses, use the money to help rebuild our business, and move on." That was a good decision. But the adverse impact of the attack on the good name of the business will take years of investment to fix.

E-mail is the hidden weapon of the web. As I write this, I am receiving e-mails from myself selling everything from drugs and gambling tips to dating sites. Our domain name SPF record (or "sender policy framework" record), an anti-spam configuration that in theory assures that the sender's address is accurate and not forged, is set properly on our firm e-mail server but obviously there are work-arounds available. I guess this particular spammer figures I'm going to get drugged up, drop some cash at the casino, and then go looking for chicks. But I'm not in Vegas, and I'm not in the market. In all seriousness, spammers have figured out that they can type any sender address into an e-mail no matter where they are sending it from. These e-mails use "false headers." How many people ignore lawyer letters? Not many. I expect this spammer is seeing some pretty good "open rates." Which means as time goes by the volume of spam "I" am sending will continue to pick up. This is a form of identity theft, defamation, and product disparagement. It's particularly problematic when those e-mails are reported as "spam" to ISPs and spam-tracking agencies.

But e-mail abuse isn't just about spammers. I've seen legitimate e-mails materially altered in a very unflattering way by the recipient and posted to the web. Some quick advice here: try sending only PDFs that cannot be modified when dealing with a sticky situation. And people love to borrow our law firm name and write official sounding letters threatening all sorts of things. It can happen to you, too. A couple of months ago I got a call from the general counsel's office of a major computer company. "Did you write us a letter, Mr. Dozier?" When I got a copy of it, I was surprised to see that a return address was included on the envelope. A quick address search led me to a state penitentiary in Virginia. I bet it wasn't the warden who sent it out. But that is just a wild guess.

On the flip side, attacks online against a business will often involve more private, intimate moments. Here's just a few I received when our law firm was undergoing a "mobosphere" attack back in October 2007. We like to read through these for laughs, but they are a good example of how e-mail traffic can interfere with your business and possibly upset your employees. And you can bet if they take the time to e-mail you they will be spouting off like this online. We got hundreds and hundreds of these in a couple of days to supplement the many telephone calls our law firm received from around the world. They are all from "anonymous cowards," of course:

"Just a flame. You're a terrible company and whoever's going through your e-mail bins and chucking out garbage should know that. Hey you, low-level clerk! Steal some important internal documents and torch the mawf*cking building!"

"You f*cking tools don't know the law from your own assholes."

"You guys are jackasses."

"Why don't you legal hacks get off the Internet until you can
learn just how outdated your profession is?"

"Retards."

"Are you tw*ts?"

"You guys are chumps . . . I'm rooting for your business to be
negatively impacted. Have a lovely day."

"I'm watching, dipshit."

"You people can't possibly, actually possess JD's. You are absolute idiots."

"Why don't you just push for banning freedom of expression?
You lawyers could make even more money if you did: "He said he
doesn't like the government" or "He tried to tell people that my company
is stealing from single mothers!" . . . What a lovely world . . . ass holes"

"You douchebags."

"I think you're a f*cking group of lawyers that will
blow anyone to get a dollar."

"You are a scumbag."

"Because you have been listed on one of the most popular
(millions of readers) blogs on the Net, your Google ranking will soon
have your bareass story on its first page of hits when somebody Googles
your firm, ha ha. My lover works as one of Google's advertising contract
lawyers, BTW, so, uh, I have a little influence at Google if you ever
try to get such listings removed, let us say."

"You are legal idiots. I will kill you all . . . "

How the heck did we get here? Do you think these types of sentiments were communicated through the printed word when the Pony Express was galloping along? We are still dealing with printed words on paper, and while the distribution systems are evolving, the nature of written communications is staying the same. Something else has changed other than the method by which communications are delivered, which we'll explore in more depth shortly.

You're Pitching on Thursday

Impersonators and Imposters

I am reminded of the story of the two elderly gentlemen who would meet in Central Park every day and while away their time dreaming of baseball. They agreed that whoever died first would go find out if there was baseball in heaven and report back. After one passed away, he returned and the surviving friend listened intently. There was good news and bad. The good news? There is baseball in heaven. The bad news? You're pitching on Thursday.

So, the good news? There is this wonderful community called the Internet that can make your dreams come true.

The bad news? Those dreams may have surprises you aren't ready for.

Twitter is a microblogging site that allows posts up to 140 characters in length. It's an interesting site allowing interesting people to constantly post comments. The attraction appears to be the ability to follow and be followed throughout the day. Even the Dalai Lama has a Twitter account. Within days of activation, he had attracted over 10,000 followers, all surely intent upon experiencing a day in the spiritual life of the Tibetan Buddhism leader. Except that his people got up with Twitter's people and reported the impersonation. Account closed.

Sounds silly, doesn't it? It would be if silliness was the limit of online impersonators. But if someone can get away with impersonating the Dalai Lama, presumably not expecting on his deathbed to receive total consciousness (if I recall Bill Murray's description in *Caddyshack* correctly), how many other imposters and impersonators are there online today?

Likely tens of thousands. And the problem is that if someone decides to impersonate you, the damage can be catastrophic. We're not talking about financial identity theft. We're addressing very real conduct that can be aimed at you, your family, and your business in seconds. The trick is that these perpetrators are focused on one thing—injuring your reputation and good name. There is no credit bureau reporting system set up to address and resolve this type of identity theft.

E-mail accounts are opened in your name and porn sent out. You are suddenly getting strange calls responding to an explicit solicitation "you" posted on Craigslist. Or your photo and other personally identifiable information are being used to open accounts on dating sites. New MySpace and Facebook profiles appear out of nowhere. How about that new website you just launched. Do you like it?

You try to open an online blog and your name is already taken. A quick blog search reveals that you already have a blog . . . with bizarre rants against your boss, coworkers, and the president of the United States, as you wonder if the next knock on the door will be the Secret Service. And you seem to be jumping into discussions all over the web making nasty comments, inciting the forum participants, egging them on, almost to the point of it appearing as if you are inviting a "mobosphere attack." And, unfortunately, "you" are.

Soon enough, your online reputation is defined by the false profiles, accounts, and comments attributed to you. But a Google Bomb has also exploded in your face. You keep pissing people off with your rants and attacking comments. They fire back in self-defense, albeit anonymously, by anchor-text linking to your crazy sites, blogging about you, and initiating or participating in a blogger swarm that will likely cause irreversible problems for you forever.

Responding to an impersonation attack can get involved. Some sites have so many impersonators that they ignore any requests for assistance. Others recognize the problem and try to deal with it proactively. This can happen to anyone; not just musicians and sports heroes. Law enforcement officers, crime victims, doctors, and lawyers are favorite subjects. MySpace even has a special complaint submission form just for teachers being impersonated.

The good news is that if you approach legitimate bloggers, they most often will remove the post. But I recall running across a rather extensive diatribe "I" authored about copyright infringement on a blog, and when I asked for the post to be removed, the blog owner claimed it had to have been posted by me since there was a link to our website in the post. The misspelling of my name was of little sway. Sometimes you run into people who are just clueless. And if "your" comments are generating a lot of dialogue, the blog owner is more likely to decide to keep it up and reap the search engine optimization and advertising benefits. Eyeballs are money, after all.

Not a month goes by that I don't hear about someone making threats or claims in my name online. Unfortunately for me, sending a cease and desist letter doesn't create a lot of goodwill. In fact, it can be the source of a Google Bomb and mobosphere attack. And it can happen to you, too.

In order to protect yourself from "yourself," set up the early warning system. Go to every major blog, e-mail, social network, social bookmarking, and reputation-related website and open a free account in your name. If you have a unique name, and you are told by the site that the name is already taken, then be very aware that something bad may be in the offing. Get all the variations of your name, your kids' names, and your business name that you can. Remember, it's free. When the attack happens, be prepared to go to websites and follow their procedures for removing content of impersonators. Be careful with the self-help, though. One of the favorite tricks used by the scofflaws involved in a mobosphere attack against your good name is to claim that you did make the comment and are now trying to retract it. Then they start attacking you for committing "fraud." It can become a vicious snarking cycle with seemingly no end in sight, itself building up more negative Google search results on your name.

Now back to the Dalai Lama. Disappointed, his legions of social networking fans are left with either his Facebook or MySpace accounts. And if they can't pull themselves away from Twitter, and still have that desire to virtually interact with a Holiness, they can go to God's personal Twitter account. Over 5,000 followers have already found God on Twitter.

ALL RISE
(REPRISED)

Twitter wasn't around in 2005, but I gladly would have taken any advice the Dalai Lama (and certainly God!) might have had to offer concerning two significant events that occurred in March and May of that seemingly endless year.

As the case had progressed, and Clark's lawyers had fought us every step of the way, the tide began to turn for some unknown reason. On March 7, 2005, Clark was sworn under oath and testified on her own behalf in Louisiana. David flew there to conduct the deposition in person and proved himself to be a skilled examiner. Under his questioning Clark admitted that although she had acquired legal counsel upon being served, she had never paid a cent to her lawyers. When asked who had been paying her attorney fees for well over a year, she denied knowing. Further questioning, however, revealed that the law firm litigating her case had direct ties (drum roll, please) to the same law firm she had sold—sorry, "loaned"—her computer to in exchange for $12,500 as compensation for the inconvenience of its brief absence.

This, of course, was the same firm that represented the large and powerful corporation that tried to silence my criticism of treatment facilities they owned by suing me unsuccessfully. Now it looked to me as if they were providing "protection" to Clark in the hopes, I believed, that she would continue to get away with disparaging my name and reputation. It's interesting that what you cannot sometimes achieve in court you can get done on the Internet.

Although Clark was receiving legal representation at no cost to herself, such was not the case with me. By May 2005, I was not only being financially drained from the cost of litigation, I was so emotionally and mentally exhausted that I felt I could not go on. But whenever settlement discussions arose, it seemed like her lawyers were never willing to get serious about them. In retrospect, I wonder now if the drawing out of this litigation was a strategy in and of itself so Clark could continue, and escalate, her attacks on me.

And so, with no other choice, I soldiered on—while the legal bills continued to mount. A rather large expense, and worth every penny, were multiple depositions taken of witnesses for me. I feel certain that these various individuals from different walks of life, whose personal and professional paths had crossed mine, played a very significant role in the fast-approaching trial—that turned out to be unexpectedly delayed.

David had spent the better part of the past year doing depositions with witnesses around the country and preparing our case in an immaculate way. We were scheduled to go to trial on July 6, 2006, as everyone returned from the Independence Day holiday. The irony was not lost on me. But then suddenly two months before trial, Clark's attorneys terminated their representation of her and the judge gave her a continuance of the trial date! As long as I had waited for justice, mine would have to wait. Whatever happened to the concept that justice delayed is justice denied? That was hard to take.

From that point forward, Clark refused to participate in the case. "Do whatever you want, I don't care," was her statement to my lawyer, before she hung up on him. She did not appear at the mediation after being ordered to do so. David continued to mail copies of all pleadings and correspondence to the address in Texas that Clark had provided to the court. The address in question was located in a gated community. Two resort pools, a putting green, fitness studio, clubhouse, business center, and more. Not exactly the Superdome.

It still bothers me that people, including lawyers who don't know about the facts of my case, claim I won because Clark had been a Hurricane Katrina victim and could not go forward with her defense. That's just total hogwash.

She would later claim to the appellate courts and in public that as a victim of Hurricane Katrina she was emotionally incapacitated, but one of her own witnesses had inadvertently revealed in depositions that Clark had sold her house about three weeks before Katrina hit. And after her lawyers fired her, she was so depressed that she moved from Texas back to Louisiana, then vacationed in Las Vegas and got married.

So it wasn't surprising to me that as I gazed around the courtroom on Monday, September 18, M. Clark was a no-show. The day I had awaited for so long, of facing her in court and making her account for herself personally to a jury, was not going to happen. But the trial would go on.

The first thing we did was pick a jury. After what seemed like forever, the judge looked at David and nodded to him to proceed with an opening statement. I was so anxious all I wanted was for the testimony to begin, but he was meticulous in carefully laying out a road map built on the details of the evidence the jury would hear. His presentation was very straightforward and matter-of-fact. But it took way too long in my mind given my almost hyperanxiety about clearing my name. It had been three long years and I was ready for it all to end so I could move on with my life. I wanted to see the jurors' reactions to my evidence, and I wanted to look them in the eyes and tell them my story. I guess I couldn't wait for someone to stand up in a position of authority and tell me that I was okay. Their word, through their verdict, is what I wanted. These were my thoughts as the opening argument consumed much of the morning.

Since the witnesses we had deposed in this case were spread out all over the country, we were able to rely on their deposition transcripts as evidence, with their testimony presented to the jury in written and oral form by David.

If you would, imagine that you're in the courtroom with me. And if you would, imagine that the testimony David is reading aloud is accompanied by the presence of each witness taking the stand under oath—an oath they all, indeed, took to swear that each word they spoke was the truth, the whole truth, and nothing but the truth. And so help me God, the last thing I would ever do is subject these good people to the very horrors I've endured by exposing their actual names in this book.

I don't know if you've already drawn a picture of David in your mind, but this is what he looks like: he's about five feet eight inches tall, not Shaquille O'Neal tall, but his presence fills up any room he walks into. He's a smart dresser, and although I've never checked the labels, he probably goes for Brooks Brothers suits when he wants to dress for success, such as this trial. Since I'm in my forties, he still seems young in his midthirties.

David is incredibly intelligent. He could be intimidating with his razor-sharp mind and quick wit if he wanted to be, but I just can't imagine him speaking down to another person—especially a jury panel that he has a way of immediately connecting with. I'm not sure if it's his pleasant voice, his animated gestures, his eye contact, his sincerity, his passion. Probably all that, and then some. I can't put my finger on what exactly it is about him that commands respect and attention almost on sight, but I'm really, really glad to have this guy in my corner.

The first witness David calls is a middle-aged woman, naturally attractive but showing the signs of stress-induced age. Adults who opt not to have children, or happen to have "perfect" children, don't wear their marching years like this. At least that's been my observation, and I've had more than my share of meetings with parents of troubled teens to draw such observations from.

"Ms. Jones," he says, "could you please tell us, how did you meet Sue Scheff?"

"At a conference in Florida on child abuse in facilities."

"And do you know what PURE is?"

"It's a little company that Sue Scheff set up to try to give parents an alternative and put their children in good programs that she has already investigated to make sure the children are safe."

"Thank you. And do you know an individual by the name of M. Clark?"

"I do. Ms. Clark contacted Sue Scheff regarding two sons who had been placed in a troubled-teen facility in Costa Rica. Ms. Scheff tried to assist Ms. Clark by giving her what information she could. And for awhile, Ms. Clark was on our listserv."

"Okay. I'm going to show you what I've marked as Composite Exhibit One, and I want you to describe to the jury what this is."

"Well, they're documents showing how we tried to help Ms. Clark and, at the ending, how angry she got when we didn't do what she asked us to do."

"And who is 'Lisa'?"

"She is the girl who was allegedly raped and beaten at the place in Costa Rica where Ms. Clark's boys were. Ms. Clark had the media there when she went to get her boys back. Then she told me through an e-mail, not through the listserv, that she had a documentary in the works on her story of getting her children from the facility they were in. She needed Lisa to come forward in order to sign a contract for this documentary."

"Was it your understanding that if she was able to get that contract for the documentary, that she would be paid money?"

"Yes, sir, that was my understanding. And she said it would be a sure deal if the victim would come forward. 'I need her to talk to the media in order to get this contract.'"

"Do you know what happened when she approached Sue Scheff to ask her to get the victim to go to the media?"

"Sue Scheff repeatedly told her the child was too traumatized and an e-mail went back and forth, and Ms. Clark's e-mails got madder and madder and said that Sue Scheff could do it. She's not helping her. Everyone on the listserve individually wrote Ms. Clark, I believe, and said it is not appropriate, the child is traumatized. She did not get angry with everyone else because she felt like Sue Scheff was the one that could get it done. Sue Scheff was holding it up. She did not feel like any of us had the authority to do it. But as you can see in this e-mail she says that she's going to do what she has to do to expose the truth."

"Did you ever have occasion to read some postings on another website besides your listserv?"

"Yes, after Ms. Clark was removed from the Trekkers, she started posting on another website, and most of her posts were directed at Ms. Scheff and PURE. The tone she used was very ugly, vengeful. She was a very bitter woman."

"To your knowledge are any of the allegations made by Ms. Clark against Ms. Scheff true?"

"Absolutely not. Mr. Pollack, I read those posts for about three to four weeks, and truthfully, they made me sick to my stomach. I quit reading them. I understand it went on for a considerable amount of time, and Sue would call me crying. She felt that it was going to hurt the kids that she's trying to help get placed because she was put in such a bad light all over the Internet. The personal attacks on her, plus the professional attacks, devastated her. She was constantly crying and went into an extreme depression. She was never like that before this happened."

"Based on your knowledge, was PURE and helping kids something that was important to Ms. Scheff?"

"It was very important to her. She lived this twenty-four hours a day. She would take calls at midnight if a parent needed something. Ms. Scheff is very dedicated to PURE and helping other parents. That's her heart."

"Now are you aware of anything that Ms. Scheff did to Ms. Clark that would have caused all of those negative postings?"

"Not what she did, what Ms. Clark assumed she did by not getting Lisa to come forward with the media or do a story. Ms. Clark lost out on any deal she was going to make, and she blamed Sue Scheff for that."

"Do you consider yourself a close personal friend of Ms. Scheff's?"

"Not a friend-that-I've-grown-up-with type of friendship, but I respect Ms. Scheff very much."

The sound of David's pause is noticeable in the courtroom. Everyone's so quiet. I have to wonder what the jury members are thinking. I still can hardly believe this all got started because of a documentary that, in Clark's mind at least, I had torpedoed—a deal that I didn't even know was in the works! Not that knowing would have changed anything. There's still no way I would have tried to push a young victim into the media spotlight for…what? Money? Fifteen minutes of fame? Okay, I finally have my answer—and I still can't wrap my brain around a motivation like that.

I keep looking at the jury, wondering what they're thinking, wondering if this day will ever end now that it's at long last here. It's been three years, *three years,* since this entire ordeal started with the threat, *"Sue, you are going down, I bet you are scared to death! You know you are going down because what you have done and are doing is wrong!"* And now that I'm having my day in court, I'm desperate for some closure, even more for vindication by a jury of my peers, as witness after witness takes the stand and the pile of documents keeps growing. Reliving all this in a room filled with strangers is painful and makes the old wounds feel so fresh. Especially when David calls Judy Davis to testify.

"Good afternoon, Ms. Davis. You've been sworn in, so you are under oath as you testify in this court. Ms. Davis, how long have you known Sue Scheff?"

"Probably three and a half years."

"And how did you meet Sue Scheff?"

"I went online after we had put our son in a program. I was doing research and I found her website. I contacted her and was basically asking her questions regarding the facilities that my son was in."

"Was she helpful in her attempt to share information?"

READER/CUSTOMER CARE SURVEY

We care about your opinions! Please take a moment to fill out our online Reader Survey at **http://survey.hcibooks.com**.

As a **"THANK YOU"** you will receive a **VALUABLE INSTANT COUPON** towards future book purchases

as well as a **SPECIAL GIFT** available only online! Or, you may mail this card back to us.

(PLEASE PRINT IN ALL CAPS)

First Name _____ MI. _____ Last Name _____

Address _____ City _____

State _____ Zip _____ Email _____

1. Gender
- ☐ Female
- ☐ Male

2. Age
- ☐ 8 or younger
- ☐ 9-12
- ☐ 17-20
- ☐ 31+
- ☐ 13-16
- ☐ 21-30

3. Did you receive this book as a gift?
- ☐ Yes
- ☐ No

4. Annual Household Income
- ☐ under $25,000
- ☐ $25,000 - $34,999
- ☐ $35,000 - $49,999
- ☐ $50,000 - $74,999
- ☐ over $75,000

5. What are the ages of the children living in your house?
- ☐ 0 - 14
- ☐ 15+

6. Marital Status
- ☐ Single
- ☐ Married
- ☐ Divorced
- ☐ Widowed

7. How did you find out about the book?
(please choose one)
- ☐ Recommendation
- ☐ Store Display
- ☐ Online
- ☐ Catalog/Mailing
- ☐ Interview/Review

8. Where do you usually buy books?
(please choose one)
- ☐ Bookstore
- ☐ Online
- ☐ Book Club/Mail Order
- ☐ Price Club (Sam's Club, Costco's, etc.)
- ☐ Retail Store (Target, Wal-Mart, etc.)

9. What subject do you enjoy reading about the most?
(please choose one)
- ☐ Parenting/Family
- ☐ Relationships
- ☐ Recovery/Addictions
- ☐ Health/Nutrition
- ☐ Christianity
- ☐ Spirituality/Inspiration
- ☐ Business Self-help
- ☐ Women's Issues
- ☐ Sports

10. What attracts you most to a book?
(please choose one)
- ☐ Title
- ☐ Cover Design
- ☐ Author
- ☐ Content

TAPE IN MIDDLE; DO NOT STAPLE

BUSINESS REPLY MAIL
FIRST-CLASS MAIL PERMIT NO 45 DEERFIELD BEACH, FL

POSTAGE WILL BE PAID BY ADDRESSEE

Health Communications, Inc.
3201 SW 15th Street
Deerfield Beach FL 33442-9875

FOLD HERE

Comments

"Yes, she was. She was well-informed and knowledgeable about it all."

"Now, have you ever met M. Clark?"

"I've never met her but I know who she is. Ms. Clark contacted Ms. Scheff because she was needing information and looking for assistance to get her sons out of a Costa Rica facility that her ex-husband had placed them in."

"Was Ms. Clark concerned about the fact that the school was in Costa Rica and she was unfamiliar with the area?"

"Yes. And I know she was taking media with her, and some other man that had been there before."

"When she decided to take these people, do you know whether that was a decision that she made on her own or that somebody forced her to do?"

"Oh, no. That was a decision she made on her own. And I sure wouldn't have gone there myself without taking someone with me. It is a foreign country, and I wouldn't know anything about it or what to expect."

"Thank you. Now Ms. Davis, what I've given you is called "Composite Exhibit One" and on page three you'll see a string of e-mails from the Trekker's listserv. Were the people who were involved with the listserv supportive of Ms. Clark in trying to get her sons out of the Costa Rica facility?"

"Yes. Everyone was trying to help Ms. Clark, not hurt her. But there was a girl that had supposedly been raped at one of the facilities, and I think it was where Ms. Clark's sons were at. And she was trying to get the girl to come forward with the rape, and she was resorting to calling and making threats to both the child and the mother. And she was doing this out of her own agenda to get this girl to go public."

"And did Ms. Clark appear to be very insistent about that?"

"She was more than insistent, yes. She was calling the mother and giving fictitious names in order to try to get them to talk to her. You know, she just wasn't honest in the beginning. Had she been honest with them, it may have been a different story."

"Do you know whether Ms. Clark at the time that she was doing this had received any offers or inquiries about participating in a documentary concerning her children?"

"Yes. It was my understanding that she was trying to use this girl's story . . . Ms. Clark was trying very hard to get this story out into the public because it would help her with that."

"Is it your understanding then, that Ms. Clark was going to be paid money to participate in the documentary?"

"Yes."

"Okay, if you'll turn to the last page, would you please summarize what these e-mails are about?"

"They're posts from the website Ms. Clark went to after we removed her from our listserv. In the different posts she's accusing PURE and Ms. Scheff of being crooks . . . being a con artist, a fraud, operating a scam . . . exploiting families and placing children in risky and possibly abusive programs."

"To the best of your knowledge, are any of those statements true statements?"

"No. Absolutely not. Sue Scheff did nothing to Ms. Clark to cause this. All Sue Scheff ever did was try to support Ms. Clark."

"Do you know whether Ms. Clark ever threatened on this website to post Ms. Scheff's deposition from another trial?"

"Yes."

"Do you have any doubt that Ms. Clark would have posted that deposition if Ms. Scheff had not gone to court to stop her?"

"I have no doubt whatsoever."

"Can you tell the jury how these negative posts affected Ms. Scheff?"

"Emotionally she was a wreck. I mean, here you have someone spreading this malicious stuff via the Internet, and she couldn't go on there and fight for herself. And then financially I'm sure that there had to be repercussions because of that."

"Do you know what kind of financial effect it had on her?"

"I shouldn't have said financially. I mean, Sue never really made a lot of money at PURE anyway. But what it did was—is put a hamper (sic) for parents to call Sue and get information, so it basically stopped Sue from being able to help, you know, children."

"Do you know whether she might have been able to help lots more children if this hadn't occurred?"

"Yes, I believe that."

"Do you know if people stopped calling her or referring people to her as a result of what these posts said?"

"Yes."

"Do you feel that Sue Scheff is different today as a result of what Ms. Clark did, in terms of Ms. Scheff's work with helping parents and kids?"

"Yes. She's extremely cautious now about who she speaks to and what she says. She would refer parents to speak to somebody else other than speak to them herself because of all this mess."

"I have no further questions, Ms. Davis. Thank you very much for your time."

And with that, Judge Luzzo declared court adjourned for the day.

I remember being beyond worn out. I remember my stomach was in knots and I hadn't eaten since breakfast, but I still couldn't take a bite out of a five-star meal if I had to. I was so drained and anxious that sleep that night was an exercise in exhaustion itself. But come morning, knowing this nightmare would be drawing to an end one way or the other in hours, adrenaline kicked in and I managed to end up at the courthouse in one piece. It was a miracle I made it since I couldn't recall a single light, turn, or other car on the road en route. But somehow there I was, along with the jury, the judge, and the bailiff, while David called the next-to-last witness.

"Good morning. Can you state your name for the record?"

"John Lewis."

"And where do you live, Mr. Lewis?"

"Pleasanton, California."

"What do you do professionally?"

"I'm retired, but professionally I was an educational psychologist with a part-time private practice and also a school psychologist."

"And in that capacity you referred parents who were looking to get information about placing their children in boarding-type schools to Ms. Scheff and to PURE?"

"Yes."

"And did you believe that Ms. Scheff did a good job in assisting those parents?"

"Absolutely."

"Based on your experience with Ms. Scheff during the eight years that you have known her, is there any factual evidence you're aware of to support that she's a crook, a con artist, or a fraud?"

"No. But let me say that after I'd referred a number of clients to her that were very pleased with her services, and in many cases they did place their children in boarding schools that Ms. Scheff and PURE referred them to, I did have a client that I referred to Ms. Scheff for consideration of placing her niece that she was the guardian of in a program. And within a few days the client came back to me very upset and asked if I was aware of all the negative things on the Internet that she read about Ms. Scheff. At the time I wasn't. And she said that she couldn't possibly call her because of all of those negative things that she read, and it turned out that the negative things were about fraud and bilking people or overcharging people and conning people."

"And that client got her information about Ms Scheff off the Internet?"

"Yes. She basically typed in either 'PURE' or 'Sue Scheff' in a search engine and that information somehow came back to her, and she was very upset at me because I was unaware of that information, or, if I was aware, I didn't inform her about it."

"Did the information that your client got off the Internet affect your decision about referring other parents to Ms. Scheff?"

"Yes. I immediately stopped referring people to Ms. Scheff and PURE, and I also removed her name from the Northern California school psychologist referral directory because I felt that it was affecting my credibility if I referred any client to anyone that had so many assailable remarks about their services that were public information."

"So those remarks affected your decision not to refer parents to PURE and to Ms. Scheff."

"Well, not only mine, but also all of my colleagues that were making referrals to PURE. There were between thirty and sixty, something like that, at the time."

"Okay, how would you describe the posts that you read in terms of their tone?"

"They were hostile, disparaging, and very negative."

"Is it fair to say that the postings caused Ms. Scheff emotional distress?"

"Yeah, absolutely. Because when she talked to me, I told her that she sounded really upset and depressed. And she said she was so depressed and embarrassed and frustrated and angry that she was really unable to continue working with families and placing their children in programs because she was so devastated by all of the lies that were being put out about her, PURE, and her daughter on the Internet; that she knew other people were reading it, and it was very traumatizing for her."

"You have had extensive experience, have you not, in your profession in dealing with parents who have troubled teens, and with people who have gone through those schools and are survivors of them?"

"Yes."

"And based on all the information that you've seen on these bulletin boards and the Internet, is it fair to say that there are a lot of parents and survivors who are very strident in their opinions about these programs?"

"Yes. And I think it's also fair to say that strident feeling sometimes is expressed in a very hostile way at other people within the community trying to help children, and Ms. Scheff was a victim of that."

"The people that you heard about those postings from, did they say that they had spoken to Ms. Scheff about them?"

"No. They basically said they knew about it and that she had lost a lot of her supporters because of those things, and that they wanted no further contact from her."

"Do you know prior to these postings about Ms. Scheff? Were people attacking her?"

"No. As a matter of fact, she was a leader, a sort of an impresario for people who needed support and consultation. Sue Scheff was always there for them. They could call her or e-mail her at any time, and in my experience, she would always provide them with very supportive, positive advice. She was a leader, someone they looked up to, someone that they wanted to help in return."

"So these posts had an effect on her reputation in the community of people involved in helping families with troubled teens?"

"They were absolutely devastating to her, to her reputation. Given the controversy and all of the consternation and negativity around PURE and around Ms. Scheff, there's absolutely no way that I could conscientiously refer a client to her."

"So even if the information wasn't really true, you still wouldn't be able to comfortably refer clients to her because it would have an impact on your reputation, correct?"

"That's a very good statement, yes."

"Okay, do you know whether any professionals outside of California, outside of your circle, were also referring parents to Ms. Scheff?"

"I know that Ms. Scheff was getting a lot of referrals from around the country because a few times I called her for consultation, and I would describe a situation or a need, and she would say, `Well, I did refer some clients to this program that I think would match your needs.' And I heard back from, you know, an educational therapist in New York or Ohio or Minnesota who said that they were very appreciative of the referral, and everything was working out well. So I know Ms. Scheff was getting referrals from professionals like me nationally."

"And had the postings on the Internet not occurred, prior to that time you were getting positive feedback about Ms. Scheff and PURE?"

"I always got positive feedback about her until that one client of mine got really upset that I didn't tell her about the things or didn't know about the controversy on the Internet regarding Ms. Scheff. The clients that I had previously referred to her were very happy with Ms. Scheff and repeatedly told me that she went over and beyond for them, that she was very helpful. And even the clients of mine that didn't place their children in schools that she recommended, she provided them a lot of consultation and a lot of referral information at no cost, and the clients were very surprised and very pleased with Ms. Scheff."

"I have no further questions, Mr. Lewis. I appreciate your time."

And now, the last witness was being called:

Me.

I honestly cannot tell you what David asked me or a word of what I said in return. Minds have a way of blocking out events we'd rather not relive. What I do remember is sitting in that witness box, unable to face my accuser of fraud and worse, so much worse, and finding some solace in the next best thing: the jury. Being able to look straight into the eyes of each one and speak directly to them in such a way I hoped they fully grasped what this moment meant for me: I had been residing in a living hell for three years, this trial period was my purgatory, and their decision was my Judgment Day.

David's closing argument was no less than brilliant. He took the vast amount of information that had accumulated over the years and made it simple for the jury to understand—the defendant was driven by greed, hatred, dishonesty, and a malicious intent. And I knew, no matter how the case came out, after hearing his closing argument I felt I *was* vindicated. I had prayed so long for someone, someplace, sometime to truly understand what I had endured. That someone was David Pollack. That someplace was before a jury of my peers. And that sometime was *now*.

The day was September 19, 2006, a Tuesday. It was a little before 2:30 in the afternoon and the weather was sunny in beautiful Fort Lauderdale, Florida. The surf was up just down the street, and my stomach was riding a wild wave as the jury of six somberly filed into the nearly empty courtroom.

I had no idea what to expect. David leaned a little closer and whispered, "Well, this is it. . . . " I wished for something I could hold onto besides his words since my legs weren't feeling very steady as the bailiff, a very kindly looking older man, intoned, "All rise."

The Honorable Judge John Luzzo, in flowing black robe and wearing his duties with appropriate dignity, took his elevated seat on the bench and asked the foreman, "Has the jury reached a verdict?"

"We have, Your Honor." She handed their verdict to the bailiff, who gave it to the judge—he nodded in seeming approval—then back it went from the judge to the bailiff to the foreman. The air was trapped in my lungs and the pound of pulsing blood was in my ears as she began to read, line by line, the jury's unanimous decision.

Suddenly I was crying and I couldn't stop the tears that were streaming down my face as David scribbled the numbers while the foreman kept reading aloud, the jury verdict form clasped in her hands. I had to see it myself, touch this paper that declared the jury's outrage over the abuse of our freedom of speech and the message they wanted to declare loudly enough to be heard around the world. Just listen:

CASE NO. 03-022837 (18)

IN THE SEVENTEENTH JUDICIAL CIRCUIT
IN AND FOR BROWARD COUNTY, FLORIDA

CIVIL DIVISION

CASE NO. 03-022837 (18)

SUSAN SCHEFF, individually and as
parent, guardian, and next friend of S.S.,
a minor child, and PARENTS UNIVERSAL
RESOURCE EXPERTS, INC. a/k/a PURE, a Florida
corporation,

     Plaintiffs

v.

     Defendant

_____

VERDICT FORM

WE, THE JURY IN THE ABOVE STYLED CAUSE, FIND AS FOLLOWS:

1.   What is the amount of any loss, injury or damages sustained by Sue Scheff in the
past as a result of Defendant's actions?

$ *890,000.00*

2.   What is the amount of any loss, injury or damages to be sustained by Sue Scheff
in the future as a result of Defendant's actions?

$ *2,535,000.00*

3.   What is the amount of any loss, injury, or damages sustained by PURE in the past
as a result of Defendant's actions?

$ *1,170,000.00*

CASE NO. 03-022837 (18)

4.   What is the amount of any loss, injury, or damages to be sustained by PURE in the
        future as a result of Defendant's actions?

                                                    $ *1,755,000.00*

5.   What is the total amount of punitive damages, if any, which you find by the
        greater weight of the evidence, should be assessed against   ?

                                                    $ *2,000,000.00 (for PURE,*
                                                    #*3,000,000.00 for Sue*
                                                                        Scheff.

If you elect not to assess punitive damage against   you should enter a zero(0)
as the amount of damages, and sign and date the Verdict Form.

                TOTAL DAMAGES OF SUE SCHEFF $ *6,425,000.00*

                TOTAL DAMAGES OF PURE $ *4,925,000.00*

SO SAY WE ALL, this *19* day of *September* 2006.

                                    Amber L
                                    FOREPERSON

The Limestone Theory

What a Court Judgment Really Means

"You can't get water from a rock" is often a self-serving declaration offered by crooks and scofflaws when caught. Obviously they never took a geology class or watched *Survivorman* get water from the most interesting places, including limestone formations through which water is filtered over hundreds of years.

It's an unfortunate misperception that exists even today. In my former life, prior to venturing off into the e-commerce world in 1994 and starting what would become a venture-backed, e-commerce solutions company recognized as the top new technology company in my region, I was a collections lawyer. Having handled hundreds of thousands of claims, and filing well over 1,000 legal actions each month, trust me when I tell you that there are many ways to collect a judgment. Because a monetary judgment carries with it consequences today that simply didn't exist before. Just as the web and Google are used to attack, they are also used to inform.

A judgment is a public record. So it won't be long before the web becomes a very effective tool for judgment creditors to list judgments and have them automatically optimized like the "product review" and "scam reporting" websites of today. This will become a form of "shaming" judgment debtors into payment, even if they have no apparent ability to pay now or in the future. For the big-money judgment debtors (Sue's experience will become more common), they will become bound by injunctions and their ability to navigate the web, and participate actively and credibly online, may be lost forever. That is going to come as a shock to those who believe there are no repercussions to ignoring the law.

Sue understands that getting an $11 million monetary judgment against someone personally is often meaningless unless it can be collected. While many homeowners may have insurance coverage under their homeowner's insurance policy, Sue's attacker did not; however Sue has retained Louisiana lawyers who are aggressively pursuing collection of the judgment. Now I have a message for the scofflaws of the web, those who think the legal system has no teeth, those who have no present ability to voluntarily pay a judgment, those who believe they can hide behind a corporation (they can't), and those who have moved all their assets overseas. Interest on an $11 million judgment is over $1 million per year. And if you think bankruptcy is an option, you are about to be very disappointed, in most cases.

The law does have teeth. My experience tells me that the majority of those who elect to undertake an online attack believe they have absolutely nothing to lose. Their response to the problems they bring on is that you cannot get water from a rock, or blood from a turnip, so you can just stand in line like all the other people who have judgments. Here is the letter I would like to write in reply:

Dear Judgment Debtor:

As you know, the judge has entered a final judgment in the sum of $1 million against you personally. In addition, there is an injunction in place prohibiting a broad range of activities. If you violate this order you can rest assured that my client will consider bringing civil contempt charges against you and referring your misconduct over to the prosecutor for consideration of criminal contempt of court charges. Despite what you might have read online, there is a "debtor's prison," and if you continue to violate the injunction my client will consider offering you the opportunity to learn the finer points of prison life.

We are going into the post-judgment collection process, during which we have an extraordinary set of tools to use to chase you down, chase your money down, chase your property down, and delve into your personal life in ways you have probably never considered. If you work, we will garnish your wages. If you have a bank account, we will take it all. If someone owes you money, we will find out and take it. You must attend depositions from this date forward every six months, during which you will bring all of your financial information, including bank account statements, and we will track down your money flow. If you have a car, we will seize it. If you have a house, we will force a court-ordered sale of it and take the equity. If you have a washer and dryer, a bicycle, a TV, and other personal property, we will send the sheriff to seize it, and we will auction your property off as advertised in your local paper.

If you get a job, we will garnish your wages within weeks. If you apply for a job, or for credit, for the remainder of your natural life this judgment will be on the first page of Google results when you are searched. This judgment will be your online legacy for your children, and the children of your children, to view forever more.

We will require you to appear in court proceedings every six months. If you fail to appear after a show cause, we can have you arrested and held in your local jail until the next hearing date. But rest assured that we will decide on the time and place of your arrest.

If you have any type of retirement account, we will make every effort to seize it. If you own stocks, we will force the liquidation and get paid the proceeds. If you run an online business, we will garnish your customers, PayPal, Google AdSense, and everyone else we can find. They will be required to pay all the money in your account on an ongoing basis to us since we will serve the garnishments every ninety days. If you move, we will follow.

This judgment will be recorded on your land records and become a lien on real estate interests you may acquire in the future. We are reporting this judgment to the credit bureaus and your ability to ever get credit again will soon be gone.

We will follow you to wherever you move, and do the same thing over and over.

The next knock on your door could be from the sheriff, and it could be anytime. But rest assured it will be at a time of our careful choosing.

Obviously this letter is a relatively succinct list of tools and remedies that, together with applicable statutory exemptions, vary by state. But you work with the tools you have. Envision yourself in the judgment debtor's shoes . . . never knowing when the sheriff will knock on his door to inventory his household effects, never knowing when the money he is owed by a business will disappear into your coffers, never knowing when he will be required to come in and be interrogated, and never knowing when his car will be pulled over and seized. Yes, you do work with the tools you have, and on a rock, I recommend a chisel.

For those of you who need a wake-up call, for those parents who want to drive the reality of online misconduct into your children's young and impressionable minds, or for those who simply need to know that our legal system is not broken but can offer powerful solutions, I write this open letter. And for those who decide to continue perpetrating attacks on the innocent, for those who embrace lawlessness over lawfulness, for those who try to wrap themselves in our flag and hide behind *OUR* Constitution, for those of you who have forsaken true justice for mob justice, and for those who have not the courage to stand up and be counted and object, but prefer rather to be swept along with the mobosphere in the latest swarm attack on the helpless, read my lips: If we get involved, we'll come knocking. And you will at that point have few options other than to live a life in destitution. Or go on the run and be looking over your shoulder for the rest of your life.

Can't get water from a rock? Think again.

The Awakening of the Sleeping Tiger

Your Time To Speak

While juries deal with individual rights and obligations, and judge on a case-by-case basis the right thing to do, the overriding societal benefit from the jury system is education. Jurors contribute mightily to defining the norms of society and what is acceptable and unacceptable conduct. They are the brave souls who toil long and hard with the singular goal of doing the right thing, and often reflect a wisdom and judgment that lawyers and judges admire and respect. And far more often than not, they get it right.

In Sue's case, they got it right. That jury could have awarded Sue some nominal amount of money. But then what message would be sent by that? Lawyers defending victims of attacks view this as a great victory, principally because it sends out a message heard around the world that the legal system is catching up with the realities of living in today's society. Lawyers for free-speech fanatics characterize the $11.3 million judgment as an anomaly, a decision of a runaway jury disconnected from reality and overcome by the passions and emotions of the moment.

Ignore it, and it will go away. Deny it, and it will be impugned. Attack it, and it will wilt.

But I am reminded of my history lessons about December 7, 1941, and the attack that will live in infamy. While the upper echelons of the Japanese forces celebrated in perceived victory, from the highest reaches of the enemy leadership came the thought that they had "awakened a sleeping tiger." Attack them and they wilt? Break their back and their will is destroyed? The attack became a defining moment when clarity of purpose was achieved and a unified will arose. And it is very much the same feeling today. Has our society evolved from being mad as hell and not willing to take it anymore to finding *Pulp Fiction* inspiration in Samuel L. Jackson's well-chosen, albeit foreboding, words? "The path of the righteous man is beset on all sides by the inequities of the selfish and the tyranny of evil men."

If so, many of you know what happened next.

Now, of course, I am not suggesting any sort of violence. This is hyperbole. And the coming struggles won't be easy. There will be skirmishes and battles and campaigns to be fought. But the war has been joined. And all across the country, in our small local courthouses to the grand halls of the Supreme Court of the United States, from the chambers of local city councils to the lobbies of Congress, justice will prevail.

But along the way reputations will be ruined. Very real dangers do exist. Those who have the courage to stand up will be threatened and attacked mercilessly. But there will come those who take this blight of online society head-on. Perhaps it will be for personal vindication. Perhaps it will be driven by a deep-seated commitment to justice, a sense of devotion to our country, or a simple fundamental belief in doing the right thing. But they will come. And one day, the scofflaws and miscreants will dig out of their caves toward the light, only to find that it is an oncoming locomotive. Yes, Sue has built the foundation for others to follow. She has paid the price. And you are soon to find out just how big a price she has paid.

BIZARRO LAND

While so much of the trial and especially its immediate aftermath is both crystal clear and spotty—a little like those zoom-in, zoom-out shots in the movies—one of the most prized memories that will stay with me for the rest of my life is how the jury came together as one and asked Judge Luzzo for permission to speak with me in the hallway after the trial.

These six people who I had never met until their selection the day before were so kind and yet so forceful in what they had to say to me that it brings tears to my eyes even now. A couple of the jurors told me that they had privately prayed about their own decision—a decision that their fellow jurors came to as well. Two other jurors told me how moved they had been by my story and encouraged me to continue my work with the families of troubled teens. Collectively they told me they had taken their duties very seriously and wanted to send a very loud message that ruining lives with online attacks was wrong and would *not* be tolerated.

And then, they *all* said they couldn't wait to get home and do a Google search on me since during the trial Judge Luzzo had instructed them that they were not allowed to look me or this case up on the Internet.

Do you have any idea, *any idea*, what this meant to me after so many years of being terrified that someone I just met would look me up and view me as a monster because they were not privy to the real facts? If these six people had done a search on me a few short days before, they would have been perfectly entitled to draw the obvious conclusions about my bad-news character. But now, these same six people could do the same search and know that almost all of what they were reading was either an outright lie or a twisted half-truth, which would now elicit anger or disgust toward my accusers, instead of that anger and disgust being directed at me, the accused.

For the first time in a very long time, I didn't feel the impulse to cringe, to run and hide, or protect myself with a knee-jerk reaction to keep the people surrounding me at arm's length. In that amazing moment I was graced. I was able to hold my head high and look each of these six people straight in their eyes without fear of condemnation.

Each juror took their turn to hug me good-bye. Each one shook David's hand. I think he was a little in awe. He said he'd never seen a trial end with such a reaction from a jury before. And, of course, once we walked out of the Broward County Courthouse and into that sweet Florida afternoon breeze, he couldn't resist a victory fist-pump into the air and an incredulous, "You just won over *ten million dollars!* Can you believe this?!"

Once alone in my car I had to take some time to compose myself. But then I had some incredible news that I was bursting to share with . . . someone. I didn't have a husband or a significant other to call.

My parents and my siblings didn't even know about the case. And, I'd kept this whole ordeal as far away from my children as possible. So, who you gonna call?

"Are you sitting down?" I asked the closest friend who had stood beside me throughout it all, and then I told her the news. At first she didn't believe me—after all, just yesterday we had seriously discussed what kind of judgment I might get, if any, and decided it could be from $10,000 to $100,000 if I was really, really lucky. Even at the upper end, it wouldn't cover my legal fees, but this had been about justice and vindication, a need so imperative that I had mortgaged my home for a chance to clear my name and restore my reputation.

Once I read the verdict to her, several times, to convince her as much as I was still trying to convince myself, she screamed. Screamed at the top of her lungs while my own were burning to do the same. Being in the courthouse parking lot, however, and not wanting someone to call 911, I reveled in those shouts of joy from a friend.

From there I went home in a euphoric daze, and just like that, the trial was over and done. Or so I thought.

Little did I realize the circus was coming to town, and it arrived with the aplomb of a two-ton elephant in a pink tutu doing pirouettes in my living room. Without warning, our quiet little landmark case hit the news and the outcome spread with viral speed.

I'm not completely sure who was the first to break the story, but before I knew it my name and the jury verdict were plastered in newspapers and magazines, on the Internet and beyond. Not just nationally but internationally. Virtually overnight I went from being a reclusive self-employed service provider getting trashed by the mobosphere to some kind of media darling/poster child for a cause célèbre that was suddenly a hot topic.

David's law office was deluged with phone calls. The phone at PURE that had stopped ringing was, in a finger snap, ringing off the hook. As for my unlisted home number, and the cell number I was stingy in giving out, well . . .

Let's just say that my father was not entirely pleased to have learned about my not-so-latest via a major spread in *USA Today*. *How could I not have told him about this? How could I have kept this all to myself when he should have been there for me?*

Boy, did I get an earful. And yet, how could I begin to explain to my father, who didn't even have an e-mail account, how treacherous and shaming an Internet attack could be? For someone who grew up in a generation when print publishers were held accountable, when the "F" word was reserved for your army buddies, and when personal matters that were meant to stay private went no further than your immediate friends and family. . . . No matter how I tried to explain this grotesque phenomenon of the Internet age, *how could he possibly understand?*

I had no ready answers for my father then. I still don't.

The first two months after the trial flew by faster than Dorothy could click her ruby slippers, and with my reputation restored on the public stage, the spotlight that came with it forced me out of hiding. I dealt with it the best that I could. I actually dealt with it better than I ever would have thought possible prior to the jury verdict. Although this was unfamiliar ground for me, although I was nervous and often unsure of myself, I found a sort of inner healing with each interview by an objective journalist in search of the truth. I also found solace and encouragement from the countless e-mails that said I had brought some much needed hope to those whose own stories of Internet abuse too closely mirrored my own.

Life had gone from really bad to better than good so quickly that

Jury awards $11.3M over defamatory Internet posts

By Laura Parker
USA TODAY

A Florida woman has been awarded $11.3 million in a defamation lawsuit against a Louisiana woman who posted messages on the Internet accusing her of being a "crook," a "con artist" and "fraud."

Legal analysts say the $11.3 award by a jury in Broward County, Fla. — first reported Friday in Daily Business Review — is one of the largest such judgments over postings

point to those who unfairly criticize others on the Internet. "I'm doesn't have $1 million ation, but the

as before returning to Louisiana last Court papers that Scheff and ney David H. Pollack were returned to

defense.

The Washington Times
www.washingtontimes.com

Lawsuit award a warning to blogs

By Kara Rowland
THE WASHINGTON TIMES
Published October 12, 2006

A Florida jury in damages defame

$11.3 million said she was board, led a Court can't

say Scheff whether to any money from "The jury determin this was a significant enough issue. It's not just somebody's feelings are hurt; it's somebody's reputation is ruined."

The Washington Post
Calling In Pros to Refine Your
Google Image

By Susan Kinzie and Ell
Washington Post Staff
Monday, July 2, 2007

At the height of consultant to p
her name in a
Up would p

Sue Scheff is des
takes kickbacks. She is
was.

The stream of negative comments began in 2005 after a woman who had sought advice from Scheff turned on her. The postings appeared on PTA Web sites in Florida, where Scheff lives. On bulletin boards and online forums. There were even YouTube videos threatening her.

Published on Asian Tribune
Internet Defamation can carry a Big Price Tag

Created 2006-10-12 13:51

Daya Gamage – US National Correspondent for Asian Tribune

Washington, D.C. 12 October (Asiantribune.com): A Florida woman who won a law a Louisiana woman, who posted messages on the internet accusing her of being a "c "fraud" said of the State of Florida's Broward Circuit Court jury award of $11.3 using the internet to destroy people they don't like, and you can't do that."

SABAH
penalty of $11 million for virtual insult
ple are

Weston Woman Wins L net Defamatic

(CBS4/AP) FT. LAUDERDALE A Weston woman who runs a business helping parents decide on school won a multi-million dollar settlement, after a court ruled she was the victim of internet defamation. I A jury has awarded $11.3 million to a woman who was called a "con artist" and "fraud" in Internet m

I was caught off guard when the spotlight I saw as vindication swerved around a blind corner and took me to a place that I can only describe as Dante's *Inferno* on LSD.

Shortly after the judgment, Clark recruited yet another ally. A former teen program attendee, this angry young person joined forces with Clark to launch an attack that would make the one I had spent years battling look like a *Romper Room* joke on *Captain Kangaroo*.

Let's call him/her . . . Alex. "Alex" is no doubt reading this book and is very disappointed that I have not granted him/her a center stage to gloat upon with an actual name and gender specification. You see, if I did, the natural inclination would be to look this person up online and, out of curiosity, explore Alex's dedicated website to me, plus the multiple links that will get you there without realizing that's where you're going. The website appears innocent enough on a search engine but once you're in, Alex's mission in life is made crystal clear: to destroy me. And, of course, each hit, unintended or not, feeds Google's hungries like the Cookie Monster getting a dump truck of Keebler goodies straight down the hatch. This delights Alex to no end.

I've never met Alex personally. All I know is that this is a very computer-savvy, sad, and sadistic young adult who apparently had something go terribly wrong in the tender years. This no doubt made Alex easy pickings for Clark to recruit to get the ultimate revenge on me for taking her to court and winning the trial she was too "traumatized" to attend once her freebie lawyers took a hike.

You know, as I'm reading that last sentence it sounds a little mean to me. To be fair, Clark surely perceives things much differently than I do, and she surely has friends and family members who would staunchly stand by her excellence of character, which I haven't had the good fortune of encountering myself.

As for Alex, I continue to search for compassion in my heart toward a disturbed individual who went so far as to . . . there are so many perversities I don't even know where to start, and it might actually be easier to give you an idea of what was coming down the pike my way by sharing an "inquiry" I received at PURE.

From: ISFORYOU@tokillyourself.com
[mailto: ISFORYOU@tokillyourself.com]
Sent: Thursday, April 10 10:29 AM

last_name: my
first_name: last dying
full_name: wish
e-mail: ISFORYOU@tokillyourself.com
re-enter_e-mail: ISFORYOU@tokillyourself.com
city: and go
state: to hell
questions_comments: your behavior in regards to Alex
makes me sick. you are despicable. you should be sent
to a program yourself.

Do I know for a certainty that Alex sent me this? I do not. It could have come from one of Alex's closest cohorts who found a picture online of my daughter and me hugging, then did a House of Horrors Photoshop job that's too sick and macabre to describe in print. Just use your imagination and multiply it by ten.

Alex's friend, Bernie, found another website where s/he secured *ten full pages* that come complete with tabloid-like headlines, copious profanity, and an assortment of news alerts that go like this:

FACT ALERT: Sue is unable to leave her house due to anonymous death threats; send her some curtains and a dog after you read this leaked email! BTW, the email was full of lies, she was never going to appear on *20/20* . . . LOL!

Actually, I did appear on 20/20, which really got the hornets' nests stirred up.

Just a few more tidbits from Bernie's little chunk of the World Wide Web:

> "Sue Scheff is a Concerned Mother and so-called advocate for them and teenagers, but in reality is a greedy Jew . . . She needs this money, of course, given that she has a crappy nose job (You can't fix a Jew nose) and obviously fake breasts, and still has payments left on her Mercedes-Benz and pool boy."

Actually, I was raised Catholic and drive an Infiniti. As for the fake breasts and the pool boy, well, ya gotta give Bernie credit for having some imaginative flair, especially since I don't have a pool and am too genetically predisposed to what I was born with to try outdoing Dolly Parton. Wait, it gets even better:

Drama, Red Panties, A Swinger, Cruella De Ville (sic), A Mormon Pedophile, and Sue-Sue F*CKS Up

Sue, being a net savvy Jew, had been lurking the boards for some time, trying to find out what people really knew about her and protecting her image. Not knowing how to handle her mistakes, she did the only thing she knew how to do: Lie, blame the victims, and generally be a f*cktard.

But the drama doesn't stop there! After Googling for porn one night she used Google to look up her enemies and more hilarity ensued when she began posting anonymously on a certain website . . . then another anon poster began making statements about Sue's red panties.

Montel Williams Fiasco

FACT ALERT: It takes a Nigra to get anything done these days

Montel could not be reached for comment, but was seen polishing a big shiny afro-pick and growing out a spectacular 'fro.

I was not on *The Montel Williams Show* but he did do a show on teen programs and their abuses, which must have qualified him to keep company with Sue-Sue.

Clark, Sue, and a Dark-Match Pollack

Having had a lot of problems with free speech, Sue needed some way to raise morale (or her sagging tits) and try to repair her image. One of her more vocal critics, M. Clark, knew full and well that Sue was full of shit, so she did the right thing and stopped the bitch in her tracks, and posted all over the f*cking internet what the bitch was up to. The image problem created by this naturally killed Sue's business. Doing the only thing she knew how to do, she hired her loser lawyer to sue M. Clark.

Being in a FEMA trailer after Katrina, Clark wasn't even able to make it to court. Being the first success Sue's lawyer ever had, he brags about it on his shitty webpage before chasing more ambulances and sucking [redacted] c*ck.

Okay. One more time: Clark sold her house three weeks before Katrina. She then moved in with the man she would eventually elope to Vegas with. While she was present for Katrina and her gentleman friend's house did suffer some damage, which caused her to temporarily move to the Houston area the next month where her parents resided, please recall that Clark independently lived in a gated community with many fine amenities. When she moved back to Louisiana to get married, she openly testified that the house she returned to— belonging to her new husband—had been repaired and was in good living order. All of this information came from Clark herself while under oath, and not once was a FEMA trailer mentioned. Got that, Bernie?

Bernie goes on to dedicate an entire page that posts an e-mail I had privately sent to a webhost provider's abuse department (more on that later), listing the police report I filed in response to threats I had received, along with David's full name and phone number. On the following page, Bernie signs off with this:

> "Not satisfied to simply send kids to be tortured for money and desperately try to fix her f*cking nose, she had to f*cking lie in the above email. Let's see if she likes what's to come? Oh and she threatened to sue me years ago, bet you wish you did now, BITCH!"

And at the bottom of the page I am quoted as saying, "Just because you don't like someone or what they do, it does not give you carte blanche to post false statements about a person on the Internet."

I did say that and stand by those words.

Speaking of words, I also received a very creepy and threatening anonymous phone call that was the same voice as the one from a

YouTube video that included pretty much everything we've already covered with the added compliment of referring to me as "a piece of human excrement," and proclaiming plans to "kick Sue's ass."

How much of a role did Alex play in all this? That's hard to say, but I'd be rather surprised if Alex's contribution wasn't significant. Even if not, as unlikely as that is, there is plenty of material that Alex is happy to take sole credit for. For example, Alex had a lengthy posting on a certain website (care to guess which one?) that lists Alex as being an administrator of it (talk about rising up in the ranks!). And on this "All about Me" sort of page, there is the same picture of my daughter and me, only undoctored, thank you. Above the picture Alex says: **"Go f*ck yourself, Sue . . . I truly hope you die in a very painful manner. Cancer preferably."**

And then there's another picture just beneath the first, with this heading: **"Sue Scheff if Alex gets his/her wish."** The picture is of a young girl in a hospital bed petting a puppy, all her hair gone and yet smiling despite the obvious ravages of cancer. Scrolling a bit further, the type reads:

> **"A rumor I heard is that Alex is on many strong psychiatric medications, still lives with his/her parents and is unemployable due to his/her psychiatric issues. How does his/her mother feel about his/her wishing death on other people?**
>
> **Will this misguided psychopath Alex finally act on one of his/her many threats?"**

And the grand finale appears in the form of yet another picture. A hand gripping a large knife and poised to strike, à la the famous shower scene in Alfred Hitchcock's *Psycho*.

There is one other item of interest that Alex mentions in this rather unusual resume on the website owned by Smith (and of which Alex is a co-administrator). Under the heading of "Experience," Alex lists "Owner/Blogger" and gives the name of the website that, at first glance, appears to be owned by me, but in reality takes you to Alex's site that is devoted to doing what Clark wasn't able to completely accomplish: Ruin me with the same sort of trash talk I took her to court for. Only now it appears that Alex is the one doing all the talking and trashing, which wasn't always the case. You see, when this website was first established, it was owned in both Clark's and Alex's names. It was only after David sent a letter of warning to the attorney Clark hired after the trial that her name was suddenly removed, leaving only Alex's remaining.

This did not stop Clark from branching out and establishing a brand spanking new website of her own, geared toward the same purpose. It's kind of like that Certs commercial: *It's Two! Two! Two mints in One!* Or maybe the old Doublemint gum jingle: *Double your pleasure! Double your fun . . . !*

It's interesting to me that while all this was going on, the media in the form of Fox News, 20/20, ABC News, the BBC, NPR, and many others continued to seek me out to shed light on Internet defamation and tell my story to the public at large. And the more exposure my story got, the more vicious the threats became. Also interesting is that when Clark lost her appeal to have her judgment set aside and was ordered to pay up, those attacks got, um, doubly bad. A last little coup de grace from Smith's website:

From Anti-Sue Scheff Guest: "Sue Scheff is evil. She is a devil and YOU SUE . . . YES YOU SUE SCHEFF—will get what is coming to you little by little. YOU WILL DIE A SLOW DEATH AND BE INFLICTED WITH

MANY DISEASES. You are an evil devil, Sue Scheff. . . . "

Clearly this all escalated to a point that made my pretrial ordeal pale in comparison. As malicious and untrue as the early postings were to destroy my reputation, they didn't involve anyone wishing me dead in graphic detail. Nor did it involve someone having my BellSouth phone lines disconnected by pretending to be me, giving them my Social Security number to prove it, and saying "I" was moving out of state. And trust me, when you're getting threats and your phone lines are cut, that's a pretty scary place to be.

I sought David's counsel. I filed a police report. I scrambled to find what avenues of protection were available to citizens like me who were given every reason to fear for their lives.

Ultimately, I called the FBI. They got involved. However, they needed more direct threats, if you can believe that, to immediately go after these sick people in order to protect one of the taxpayers who cut their paychecks. And why? Because under the current, existing laws with the Internet, nothing entirely illegal was going on. As John has made clear from a legal perspective, our present laws are not only grossly inadequate, they are geared more toward protecting the guilty than the innocent when it comes to online stalking and abuse.

With my options running out, and my *Fear Factor* mounting, I went in search of help. Where? Where else:

The Internet.

Circling Sharks

Sucks Sites

Sue is feeling the brunt of an attack site aimed squarely at herself personally and her business. This is not uncommon. It's becoming a very popular pastime among the disenfranchised. Now, don't get me wrong. No one would seriously dispute the right to voice honest discontent with a company or individual. This right to free speech is planted firmly in our history and protected in the First Amendment to our Constitution. It's as American as apple pie.

But if someone decides to buy your business name with a derogatory term attached, like "sucks" or "stinks," and offers up to the search engines a less than flattering page title, the site will likely be presented in a Google search result with the title as the headline. And when that prospective customer, employee, or vendor sees this shocking headline and clicks on the link to this web page, they'll be reading about all of your skeletons in the closet. If the content is truthful or mere opinion it is often quite legal, although I'll explain shortly how existing privacy laws may even make true statements illegal.

In the early days of the Internet, the information on these sites was most often an expression of displeasure with the business for some objectively factual reason. Or pure statements of opinion. So, if you think that our president sucks, you could say so. If you think that your local dentist sucks, you can say so. If you think your brother's employer sucks, you could say so. I don't recommend you do so for a number of reasons, both legal and practical. You could get sued by someone who is offended and misguided. Or you could be attacked by those who disagree with your view. Although your speech is likely protected free speech, always remember that the free-speech expansionists are ready to attack your speech, and your right to speak, at a moment's notice if they disagree with you. It is the irony of ironies, no doubt. But that philosophy lives a vibrant life online. I call sites used for legitimate purposes such as these "gripe sites." They are the instruments by which we, as a free people, voice our opinions. And the courts have developed a long history of protecting these sites and their owners.

Public-interest groups have played an important role in protecting our civil rights over the years. And protecting the public's right to criticize became a main objective at the turn of this century. Preserving our free speech rights, maintaining open access to information distribution systems like the Internet, promoting government and business accountability and transparency, and preserving a healthy "marketplace of ideas" are worthy causes. These public-interest organizations served the role of legal counsel to many of the original "gripe" sites, and when invited into court by a targeted business, regularly won cases. They were seen by netizens as darlings of the Internet and protectors of the masses. These groups used the attention and publicity to raise money in order to keep fighting the good fight and turned "gripe site" protection into a cash cow. A money-making machine. Not widely known at the time was the developing practice of payoffs being made by targeted businesses to stop the negative comments. Perhaps the comments were true. Perhaps they were not. But they were hurting the business targeted.

Businesses began buying the domain name and website for a handsome sum or hiring the website owner as a consultant to get rid of the negative comments. The entire process had evolved into straight out blackmail and extortion. Legitimate complaints were morphing into half-truths and innuendo, and those eventually evolved into outright lies. And when the even more nefarious netizens from all around the world saw how profitable this attack-site business could be, they began watching very closely. The sharks of online society took notice, and they wanted in on the action. Because they saw how easy it was to buy a domain name, launch a "gripe" site, get free lawyers, and get paid off. These virtual sharks soon realized that the bigger the damage to a business or professional, the bigger the payout. So they started launching sites that were full of lies, sites that would siphon off business customers directly to a competitor, sites that were fronts for commercial websites, sites that were themselves carrying cash-generating advertisements, and sites that were so highly and expertly programmed that they would be one of the first results when someone searched Google for the target. I call these "sucks sites." And suck they do.

While they may appear to most visitors to house legitimate complaints, they are all too often money machines and cash cows. They are often driven by greed, not principle. The owners of "sucks sites" are not the least bit concerned about legitimate customer complaints or factual and fair business reviews. All they care about is our First Amendment and how it can be used to hide their illegal ways.

As these sharks circle a target, the public-interest groups hop a tourist boat and go out for the show. The first frenzied attack begins, and as the boat motors into the fray, many of these free-speech tourists sit back in their chairs, sip their drinks, soak in the rays, and watch intently as their buddies toss buckets of chum over the side. They've got to make sure there are plenty of sharks in the water. After all, there is protection in numbers. And the public-interest and free-speech and consumer-rights groups are there to offer protection as long as the contributions keep coming in. This bait is expensive stuff, you know.

Today the consumer-rights groups are extremely active in protecting all sorts of sharks, from the hammerhead to the great white, and continue to offer guidance, support, cover, and free lawyers. Having overlooked, quite by accident I'm sure, the fact that their shark clients of today are threatening the very rights to legitimate free speech that they had fought so hard to protect and preserve. It's all about greed. And it's sad.

Just as surely as the courts initially embraced the honorable intent and public benefits of the original "gripe sites," the tables are turning. Because of these abuses, no legitimate gripe site will be afforded the benefit of the doubt. Motivations will be questioned, suspicions will run rampant, innocent explanations will be discounted, heartfelt guidance will be viewed with jaundiced eyes, and the truth will eventually out. When that happens, our right to free speech will be diminished in one sense but ultimately strengthened in another, more constructive way.

In the meantime, these sites will become increasingly dangerous attack vehicles aimed at crippling a business or ruining a reputation. For a price, the problem can often be solved. If your business is under attack, you should consider this as a possible solution. Many businesses we represent make this very difficult decision to pay the extortionist and have the matter over with. A second possible solution is to use "search engine optimization" techniques to get the site moved out of harm's way on the Google search results. A third option is "self help" . . . go to the webhost, the domain registrar, Google, or the likes, and plead your case. Another option is to file a lawsuit or pursue other legal action. All of these are risky, time-consuming, or costly. Possibly all three. That's why the sharks are there. If there was an inexpensive or easy exit strategy, the sharks and their lawyers would be out phishing for something of a different sort.

Pajamas and a Toothbrush

Cyberstalking

"I'm being cyberbullied." That is what I often hear from a prospective client. I'm sure Sue was feeling that way throughout her ordeal, particularly as things escalated into death threats after the jury verdict. Technically it's a misnomer, though, since cyberbullying usually refers to bullying involving juveniles. Sue is experiencing "cyberstalking." And Sue's story has plenty of cyberstalking-type conduct to get the attention of the authorities. So why aren't some of these people being prosecuted criminally?

Let's avoid getting into some kind of a deep legal analysis of what communications are necessary to bring about stalking charges. The fact is that most states do have criminal stalking laws. Most of those laws have civil aspects to them, which means a judge can issue civil remedies like TROs (temporary restraining orders) and injunctions prohibiting the stalker from further contact. But there is no federal law with any meat on the bone. That means that it is up to the state prosecutors to chase these characters, and when the perpetrators are out of state, most prosecutors won't fool with the matter. There might be some federal laws that could be used when real threats of physical harm, coupled with an immediate ability to carry out those threats, exist. But when it comes to online cyberstalking, the FBI can't commit its resources to chasing some computer geek so far away that the chance of the stalker doing any real physical harm is very low. Local police often insist that the stalking law requires an imminent threat of physical bodily harm, but in many instances that law has changed, and I suspect the ignoring of such is sometimes used as an excuse not to get involved. Frankly, one can understand the need to prioritize if you are running a police department and chasing murderers, rapists, and robbers all night long and worrying about national security during the day. But priorities do need to change.

So what can you do? You may have an invasion of privacy claim, or you may not, given the chaotic state of those laws which I will shortly address. California, notably, not only has a criminal law, but has created a "tort of stalking." That means a victim can sue for an injunction and compensatory and punitive damages in California. Unfortunately, the tort requires that the stalker engage in a pattern of conduct the intent of which was to harass the plaintiff, and the plaintiff must reasonably fear for her safety. Compare that to the exclusively criminal state laws that simply require a person to intentionally cause a reasonable person to be seriously alarmed, annoyed, or harassed. It looks to me like the strongest laws are criminal, and no one wants to waste the time and money to prosecute. And the civil laws that allow victims to sue on their own are few and pretty weak. That needs to change.

Congress should pass a national tort of stalking law that will allow you to file a lawsuit in federal court. States should pass laws that do not require a real and present threat to physical safety and allow civil lawsuits to be filed. The damages recoverable should be compensatory damages, punitive damages, triple damages, and attorneys fees, and simplified processes for obtaining broad injunctive relief should be established.

I've seen the stalking effect up close and personal and appreciate the irrationality involved. It is hard to understand how someone can become so obsessed and throw caution to the wind. When I first started practicing law twenty-eight years ago I represented a young man who was following his ex-girlfriend around and threatening her. The judge deferred deciding the case, continued it for six months, and ordered that he stay away from her. After the hearing I finished up my cases, returned to the office, and picked up my messages. One was from the court clerk. On his way out of the courthouse, my client decided to visit with the victim. He was in jail, the clerk advised, and the judge was pissed.

As I approached the bench the following morning, the judge did not look up from his papers, except to ask me if my client had brought his pajamas and toothbrush. "Why?" I asked. "Because he's going to jail" was the reply. And several months later, after my client served his time, I found myself before the same judge again with the same client. He followed my suggestion and brought his pajamas and toothbrush. This time as we walked up the center aisle of the courtroom the judge looked up, saw my client carrying his gear, and smiled and nodded in approval. If only it was that easy with cyberstalkers.

Do you realize there are serious state and federal civil business laws dealing with copyright, trademark, trade secrets, and business conspiracies that carry enhanced damages and simplified injunctive procedures? Yet next to nothing for stalking. These laws need to be passed. The local police department and prosecutor are not going to make stalking cases a priority for criminal prosecution. The FBI is not going to spend its time investigating a bunch of "personal problems." We need laws that make it easy to sue harassers and shut them down. And while the legislators are at it, they can make sure the new laws cover stalking-by-proxy, which is an element of a mobosphere attack and involves getting others to do the dirty work for the stalker. From the look of things, Sue is a victim of this. It's a kind of conspiracy. Having read Sue's story, you have a very good idea how this stalking conspiracy works.

Are Citizen Journalists Either?

Online Legal Advice

Sue is experiencing an attack from those who are considered "citizen journalists." Real journalists hate them. Real citizens hate them. But they love themselves! Citizen journalism is news and commentary from the public at large. The sources include bloggers, social network participants, website owners, and everyone voicing their opinion on a topic online. Everyone's a citizen journalist. But most people online reject this concept and likely appreciate that this label is a self-anointment of prestige or importance by those who believe everyone should be equal in importance and authority. That's the democratization theme coming through again. The motive, though, is to steal from real journalists the shield laws and other legal benefits real journalists enjoy, and ride on the backs of the traditional press who have fought so hard to preserve the right to legitimate free speech. And a good number embrace the newly minted label because it's easier to convince sports teams they should get press credentials.

When will we have "citizen lawyers," "citizen doctors," and "citizen nuclear engineers"? It seems a natural next step. And a stark and clear way of putting in perspective the harm that can come from this theft of the hard-fought rights earned over centuries by legitimate journalists. Armed with this new persona, this new badge of honor and courage, these citizen journalists convince themselves that every word they type is protected by free speech and they have an obligation to pursue the truth in all things that catch their fancy. The fundamental problem is that they often have not the slightest concept of free speech or truth. But they do have a voice and their words are, if nothing else, getting attention. So that justifies everything a citizen journalist publishes. The more outrageous the claim, the more traffic flows to the site. That's a fact of life in the online citizen-journalist world and often is the primary motivation. Do Sue's attackers truly believe in some weird way that they are doing the public a service by warning everyone about Sue? It is likely a very common thought for those who decide the ends justify the means, but true motivation is hard to decipher in online attacks. Perhaps the end to them means total destruction of their target. These types are sometimes serial attackers and will then simply move on to another target. And some attack on many fronts at the same time.

Ronald J. Riley, the owner of the "sucks site" aimed at our law firm, has his hands in sucks sites all over the place, and once got sued for his online attack of his daughter's public school teacher and Girl Scout leader. He is the ultimate serial "citizen journalist," and, not surprisingly, has a close relationship with consumer-rights lawyers going back almost eight years. There are also a remarkably large number of these people who believe that if property is on the web, it is free for the taking. Information yearns to be free, they believe. And there is some truth to this mantra voiced all over the world. But all information is not meant to be free.

Movies, songs, poems, books, and other creative works aren't meant to be free. And for that reason, in order to promote creativity, we afford certain legal protections to the owners. The legal doctrine is copyright. Consumers can enjoy these things because our copyright infringement laws benefit creators of the works. Otherwise, few innovative and creative endeavors would be pursued.

A business name like Exxon or Coke or Microsoft isn't meant to be free for the taking either. So the legal doctrine of trademark protects not only business names, but service and product names. Otherwise, consumers would be unable to distinguish between high quality products and inferior or even dangerous alternatives.

Free speech isn't entirely free. Disclosing certain types of private information, even if already public, could be against privacy laws. And the passing of false information is addressed by our defamation laws. If consumers are misled by lies, they are precluded from making smart, informed decisions.

If you really think about it, all of these legal protections benefit the citizen consumer. Because if everyone could have free access to movies, if everyone could use any business name for a product label, and if everyone could say whatever they wanted about anyone else, our society would lose the ability to enjoy creative works and make informed decisions. We would become a cauldron of deceit; a cesspool of dishonesty. Our freedoms would ultimately be at risk.

And today in the online world it is fair to say, I think, that society's freedom is being stolen by crooks.

Part of the problem, a big part of the problem, is ignorance. The conduct of the web is governed by laws. Now, you won't find a code of ethics out there, at least not one that is taken seriously or followed. But a quick search on any legal subject will lead you to the legal guidance from "citizen journalists" whose advice is a product of no legal training and a hidden agenda. Some of the advice is comical and would be funny if not offered up on a highly popular website with many rabid followers. Here are some examples of online legal "advice":

• Just preface all of your attacks against a company or person with "In my opinion" and you can't be sued.
• If you buy your competitor's domain name and "park" it, you are legal.
• "Fair use" allows me to use someone's video or photograph or business name commercially.

These tips come from otherwise credible "citizen journalists" with not the slightest legal training. People actually believe this stuff, and then it gets repeated so often by them and others that it seems to become the law of the web among nonlawyer netizens.

Citizens of the web just don't know better because they are being taught by self-styled "citizen journalists," many of whom are consumer-rights extremists, free-speech expansionists, and antibusiness propagandists. Here's a short piece of advice for "citizen journalists." Gain a balanced perspective on the legal code of conduct for your online activities.

The Streisand Effect and the Virtual Hydra

Conspiracy and Hacking

Sue hasn't covered all of the spin-off attacks spawned by the jury verdict. But people everywhere were getting involved. The desire to take a look is nothing new. Who among us has not slowed down to see if we can get a peek of that car accident? But the Internet supercharges things . . . and, in Sue's case, these gawkers are all offering their rather graphic derogatory thoughts about the judgment and Sue.

The Streisand Effect is the process and impact of a mobosphere attack. But how does a single online post or blog lead to a seemingly coordinated, and certainly overwhelming and often devastating, assault? Through sheer momentum, in part, but more so through the common interest of online scofflaws in making sure that everyone knows who is boss when it comes to controlling the web. It's as if there is lingering in the depths of the web an online version of the Hydra of Greek mythology. Online mobs often operate as one, using various websites to discuss, plan, implement, and then brag about the use of the many weapons we have discussed. They often operate like the mythical snake with many heads, spewing deadly poisonous breath.

So while the Hydra breathes poison and attacks using its many heads, so, too, do the scofflaws populating the mobosphere. From all directions come stalkers, hackers, spammers, liars, extortionists, and copyright and trademark thieves, all offering up their own devastating poison and dropping far more than Google Bombs. Fire-breathing dragons would never have a chance against this crowd of one with many heads. And while most defamatory attacks target their victims through words only, I've gone to war with my share of Hydras. While most consider the Streisand Effect to be the process and result of a war of words and battle of intellect, the truth is that the real Streisand Effect implicates attacks against victims far beyond mere speech.

One of the most memorable Hydra attacks (for obvious reasons) was against our law firm.

It had been a long day in San Jose, California, as I returned to my hotel room. I ordered room service, went to my laptop, booted it up, signed into our remote server, and stared at e-mail after e-mail laced with profanity. As I opened the Google alerts that had been flowing in all day, I was seeing comments all over the web about our law firm's supposed claims of owning HTML—the very computer code used to program most web pages. As I started deleting all of the anonymous e-mails, I decided to check my voicemail back at the office. It was full of messages from interesting characters demanding a return call to discuss our claim that we own the Internet. While I'd like to think that our voice has contributed to the maturation of our online society, I didn't invent the Internet. And I didn't own any rights to HTML source code. As I went to bed that night in Silicon Valley, I wondered what my office on the East Coast would be facing first thing the next morning.

I set my alarm for 4:30 AM. I was still on East Coast time, thank goodness. Our receptionist reported an onslaught of calls to other attorneys in the office from really strange people. An e-mail popped up from our webhost inquiring about the dramatic increase in traffic, and I was soon to learn about getting "slashdotted." The volume of visits to our site was growing by the thousands before our eyes as our technical people allocated more capacity. We were seeing visits from around the world. Even with the increase in the size of our connection, our website became overwhelmed.

Later, as I have mentioned previously, we would find out that hackers posted a Britney Spears video. At about the same time, a hacker posted images of child pornography in the administrative area of our website, bragging about his hack. Fortunately, none of our internal law firm systems were compromised because those are heavily protected and not connected to our public website. But what had begun as a Google Bomb, a bunch of bloggers criticizing our law firm and linking to each other's sites with our law firm name to make Google present negative results when we were searched, had evolved into a Streisand Effect-fueled visit from the Virtual Hydra.

The Google Bomb technique had worked masterfully. Now all of the criticisms were coming up on the first and second page of results when someone searched for our law firm on Google. Bloggers started keeping score, ranking the derogatory search results each week like a college football poll, relishing the devastation to our reputation and Google Bombing us over and over again.

We've discussed Google Bombs, the Streisand Effect, and the Virtual Hydra. Notice that each requires many same-minded participants. No one today seems to understand, appreciate, or acknowledge the illegal implications of these conspiracies that are often coupled with defamation, hacking, child porn, trademark infringement, copyright infringement, extortion, and RICO (Racketeer Influenced and Corrupt Organizations) violations. For those instigators, organizers, and counselors participating in the mob but so ready to claim innocent ignorance, you may get away with it. But if an attacker is found out, the consequences could very well be life-altering. Like an $11 million judgment and notoriety so widespread that the hope of gainful employment will be a pipedream if not a nightmare. One day the attackers will be cornered, left cowering and begging for forgiveness and conciliation. But the web remembers. For generations.

Nice legacy.

And that is exactly why Sue is fighting so hard against the new wave of attacks. More fronts will soon open against her. Some expected. Some totally unexpected. All very, very damaging. But the question remains: where is she to go when the only true protection comes from the Internet itself?

HOW THE WEB IS WON

Since the legal authorities were no help, and I couldn't, and of course, wouldn't, exactly turn to Tony Soprano for some protection against the online threats being made against me, a friend to whom I will be forever grateful advised me of a new company that offered protective services to individuals and businesses who were victims of Internet attacks.

In the past few years, more such service companies have emerged, and while I'm sure that many of them are excellent, and John can probably tell you about some of them, my sole experience is with ReputationDefender, founded by Michael Fertik. I want to tell you about ReputationDefender and Michael because they rescued me when I was frightened and desperate and had no where else to turn. No doubt I am biased in my opinion toward Michael and his group— and who wouldn't be after the above-and-beyond lengths they have gone to on my behalf.

First, a little about Michael. After graduating from Harvard and then Harvard Law School, rather than try court cases, he decided to try his hand as an Internet entrepreneur—with the idea that he would return to law after he explored an area of Internet inequity he felt very passionately about. The inequity centered around his observation that an individual's right to privacy had been corrupted by the unrestricted flow of biased or false information presented as truth on the Internet, often with devastating consequences to innocent individuals.

In response, he established ReputationDefender in the spring of 2006 with a small team of other young brainiacs like himself. A few short years later he has over fifty employees and travels the world to meet with clients. I think Michael's plans to turn his professional attention back to law may be indefinitely delayed.

Anyway, in December of 2006, I initially contacted Reputation-Defender with an e-mail. I was hopeful, but didn't dare get my hopes too high.

Within twenty-four hours I received a personal phone call from the CEO himself. Michael had me at "Hello." He calmed me down with equal measures of techie logic and human compassion. His empathy was something I desperately needed, and I have no doubt as to just how deep that empathy truly goes. There are a lot of Clarks and Smiths and Alexes and Bernies in the cyberworld, and by protecting the reputation of others like myself, he risks retaliation from a thwarted online thug. Michael has donned one of the biggest XXXL orange sweaters with a target on the back.

As promised, after our initial phone call Michael researched my case and once convinced of its authenticity, he and his team at ReputationDefender immediately, and aggressively, began pursuing the sites and blogs that were spewing hate talk and vile things about me. These sites were quite successful in their intent to destroy me since they commanded the first few pages of Google results for both Sue Scheff and PURE. But once Michael came on the scene, within a few months those same pages *turned up unblemished results*. It was like rewinding the clock to more innocent days, when I was minding my own business and everybody else was minding theirs. Only now there was evidence that we can never turn back the hands of time: The prolific number of news articles attached to my name was proof positive that Dorothy might have gone back to Kansas but Oz was indeed real, and she would never be the same.

While there's no changing the past, Michael's expertise made some drastic changes to both my inner and Internet images that were good for the soul . . . and a good night's sleep. He managed to push the malicious commentary down so far and the real me up so high on Google, that I could almost forget there were people out there who would love nothing better than to see me dead. In fact, my confidence had moved up so much as a result, I got brave! When I was approached to publicly discuss my case, I wanted to give credit where credit was due. While David Pollack had been my champion in the courtroom, Michael came to my rescue after the case was over, and I appreciated the opportunity to say so when reporters called. And call they did, from distant lands and respected periodicals that a year before I never would have imagined being quoted in:

Forbes, the *Wall Street Journal*, the *Washington Post*, even the *Peninsula*, which is "Qatar's Leading English Daily." Actually, I wasn't sure where Qatar was on the map, so I did a Google search and found out it's a peninsula in the Persian Gulf that's bounded in the south by the United Arab Emirates. Yes, it's still amazing to me how much can be learned with a few words typed into a search engine.

One of my favorite articles was from the *San Francisco Chronicle*. It appeared on Sunday, May 6, 2007. The reason I like this so much is because it illustrates how out of control this cybersmearing has gotten, how I am so not alone. A good part of the article is dedicated to discussing some young Yale female law students who were "singled out by anonymous contributors to a popular law school message board." How ironic that as I was writing this, John sent me a just-published *Condé Nast Portfolio* article (March, 09) titled "Slimed Online" that tells how two of these girls were Google Bombed in the most horrible of ways and have now publicly filed a lawsuit against these "anonymous" trolls. The story also reveals how Michael offered his assistance and went after the website that was generating the vitriolic attacks.

I love Michael's headline quote: **"The Internet is a big tattooing machine that makes you relive momentary mistakes and lapses in judgment that we all make."**

Unfortunately, I would soon learn how terribly true and prescient his statement was. After those articles went to print and appeared online, my enemies started escalating their combined energies to counteract ReputationDefender and slime me. They also started attacking a good friend for no reason, and I felt extremely guilty about that. I had a sinking sensation of going under again and felt I needed to do something, so in my newfound confidence I personally went after my online nemeses and sent a letter to the "spam and abuse department" at a webhost provider who hosted the site where Smith's website was parked.

I provided the evidence (which wasn't hard to produce, that's for sure) that Smith was breaking their "terms of service" and "code of conduct" and asked them to remove Smith's site. The spam and abuse department, in turn, confronted Smith with the letter I had sent requesting their removal. And in that letter I made a major mistake by mentioning that I was soon scheduled to appear on 20/20 with regard to this very type of Internet abuse.

Well, as soon as Smith and her cronies got a gander at that, don't you know that ABC was swamped with negative e-mails and calls about my upcoming appearance? And, since I had gone public about how Michael and ReputationDefender had rescued me, Alex realized how I had managed to outsmart them and committed him/herself with a fanatical fervor to finding a way to restore their hate talk to the higher rankings on Google.

From there, it was like dominoes falling, and fast.

The 20/20 program was scheduled to air on August 14, 2007. On August 7, exactly one week prior, Alex and Clark established the website I mentioned earlier—the one that appears to be owned by me but takes you straight to my online version of hell (Alex is probably throwing the confetti and whooping in glee right now). And, by the morning of the 14th, not only had Smith's website gone berserk with their threats and death wishes and sliming, Alex had found a way to bounce his/her and Clark's website up to the first page of Google's results. Frantic, I sent an e-mail to Michael filled with my devastation over what seemed to be a déjà vu plunge into the beginning of the whole nightmarish ordeal all over again. His response, as always, was finger-snap quick:

From: Michael Fertik
Sent: Tuesday, August 14, 2007 9:53 a.m.
To: Sue
Cc: [redacted]

You're a very brave lady, Sue! By speaking up, you are giving confidence to thousands of people who have been victimized the way you have. We'll keep working on this till the cows come home for you. The main thing for us to do is to keep plugging away. We've beaten back two of their waves already (remember how bad it was in December?), and we'll beat them again for you. There will be more fallout, as expected, after tonight, and it will take time to improve it all again, but we'll get it done for you. [redacted], we're doing a couple press releases today, right? *Michael*

————Original Message————

From: [redacted]
To: Sue
Subject: Good Morning!

Good Morning, Sue!

Looking at things this morning, it seems that we are in decent shape. A few things have been pushed down, and I will be publishing two excellent press releases this morning about you through numerous PR sources!

Thank you for pitching in so much over the past days; having YOUR voice will be great when even those who see the negative articles also see that you have chosen the high road in this fight.

As you can see, Michael tried to calm me down and build me up while making sure his team members were beating back the negativity with positive PR. And as you can also see, his eager associate, sweet as she could be, was earnestly trying her best to get those "two excellent press releases" published far and wide. And she did a superior job at it. However, given my state of mind with appearing on a major TV show for the first time and the possibility of so many viewers deciding to do a Google search on me, I made "a momentary mistake" and a lapse in judgment that truly, anyone could have made, which I am reliving to this day.

I did not review the press releases before they went out. One of the press releases contained a misquote stating that my organization didn't make a profit and our services were free. Yes, our services *are* free to the families who seek out PURE, however schools and programs do cost money and some of them do pay us, definitely not all of them, or I would be driving around in a Bentley and most likely would have that pool guy. So yes, we do have some income, but not in the way Smith and Alex and Clark and their minions so insistently and loudly proclaim it to be.

The thing about having cyberstalkers is that they follow your every move, every keystroke, and are there to "catch ya" for even the tiniest mistake made. I made a mistake by not reading that press release. I should have taken a magnifying glass to it before ever letting it go out. But I didn't, and as soon as I saw the error a couple of days later, I contacted the associate who had written and sent the releases out. Even though I took accountability for the glitch, she was profusely apologetic and *immediately* yanked the press release from distribution—but not before Alex screen-captured the misquoting. Even to this day s/he uses it as a screen signature sign-off . . . with a little editorial commentary, Alex-style: "As a free, non-profit service, we provide a haven for truth and reality —*S. Scheff (fu-kin surreal)"*

For the life of me, I have no idea what any person could gain from an obsession like this. Whatever the motivation, Michael has dealt with some pretty sick stuff far beyond my own circumstances. Perhaps you've heard of the Nikki Catsouras case? She's the young girl, eighteen years old, who snuck the keys to her father's sports car, put the pedal to the metal, went across a median and into a toll booth. She was decapitated. Her family was instructed not to view any of the police photos from the resulting carnage. Their beautiful daughter was mutilated, unrecognizable. And although Nikki's parents and siblings abided by that directive, someone got hold of the police photos and posted them online. They went viral. Pictures of Nikki's decapitated body eventually appeared on 1,600 websites in fifty different countries.

20/20 did a special on Nikki's family and the macabre aftermath they experienced after the unthinkable happened. Nikki's mother explained how she had approached one of the websites and begged them to take down the gruesome pictures of their daughter. The website refused, citing constitutional protections and their free-speech rights. It's as if there are no longer any invasion-of-privacy rights, just like John has previously discussed. *But we have rights, too,* this mother told the reporter. Nikki's father, a real estate agent, opened an e-mail addressed to him that appeared to be a legitimate business inquiry just a few weeks after Nikki's death. And there to greet the grieving father were these words: *"Dead Girl Walking. Ooooh, Daddy, I'm alive."*

When the Catsouras family couldn't take it anymore, they hired Michael Fertik to get Nikki's pictures off the web. Michael admits in the interview how extremely hard this case has been to completely succeed with due to the proliferation of the images. He likens them to a malignant cancer; he no sooner gets them off one website than the images spread to others. This is the Streisand Effect in action, as John would point out, a mob without a conscience descending upon a selected target and going forth to multiply their ugly agenda en masse.

From my own personal experience I can say with conviction that I believe if anyone can help the Catsouras family protect themselves, it is Michael Fertik. Such heroics can come at quite a cost. Does Michael have "sucks sites" and negative blogs against him? Sure he does. But the way he looks at it is, "Sometimes you find yourself in the firing line, on the unhappy end of an attack, but you know what? It's the cost of doing business in my field and those are scars that I'm proud to bear. I can suck it up and take a few body blows for clients who I feel don't deserve that kind of abuse."

While no one beats Michael as the best, at least in my eyes, I would be remiss if I didn't acknowledge that there are other webhost providers, press release service providers, and websites that stood up to be counted amongst the "good guys" of the web for insisting that their "terms of service" and "code of conduct" policies be honored by those who seek their services. They removed Smith's and Alex's web-sites and postings due to their slanderous and threatening content. But these reputable entities did nothing more for me than they would do for anyone else who can prove one of their clients is behaving with malice and a complete disregard for the code of conduct they agreed to upon signing up, and are expected to abide by in exchange for the services provided.

It's called respecting the rules of their virtual turf. Of course there will always be people who would rather break rules or bend them beyond a reasonable extension, and I'm far too well acquainted with some of those individuals. Recently I discovered that Clark created a Google AdWords campaign so that she set up sponsored advertisements on Google with my name—a name I have now trademarked—and whenever anyone clicks on the ad, straight they go to her website, not mine! Another good guy to the rescue, who will remain unnamed, made sure Clark's ploy was shot down and the Google advertisements disabled.

Alex continues to be a thorn in my side, but I am aggressively pursuing the dismantlement of his/her very mean trick of the Internet trade. My sincere hope is that by the time you read these words, this will be a nonissue. If not, stay tuned. I'm determined to see justice done with that one.

Fortunately, I have some very fine people of high moral, ethical, and professional ilk who have my back, orange sweater with a target on it and all. Hats off to the men and women of the Internet who bring some desperately needed standards of integrity to the Wild, Wild Web.

First and Lasting Impressions

Google AdWords Advertising

Sue is now seeing the misuse of paid advertising as an attack tool. Fortunately, the problem was taken care of quickly. That is not always the case, though. When you are faced with this problem, go to Google first and see if they will pull down the offending advertisement before considering other options. Let's spend a moment on Google AdWords.

How would you like it if I told you that the first thing someone sees when they search for you or your business is under your total control? After all we have discussed about the battle for the first page of Google results in reputation management, I expect you might be surprised. But it is true. You can have the first result and guarantee someone searching for you will have a positive first impression. But before I go into this in detail, let's understand a little more about why Google is the leading reputation engine and why the small monetary investment may be worth considering.

As we've seen, Google is the reputation engine at the center of attention. If you have been over to Yahoo you'll notice dramatically different search results. Yahoo seems to give preference to the tried-and-true websites and more traditional web properties. It appears to emphasize established information and traditional authority structures, some of the strongest indicators of the "rational" left hemisphere of the brain. Google's results, on the other hand, are more intuitive, seem to rely on hunches and seek out patterns, are fluid and spontaneous, and prefer a more collegial authority structure. That's the right side of the brain speaking.

Since online attacks are much more likely to target Google criteria for authoritativeness and relevance (which places a premium on spontaneity, hunches, uncertainty, and authority by popularity rather than merit), they show up much more prominently on Google. The attackers know this. And since Google is the most popular search engine with monster market share, it rules. The effect of a bias toward the democratization of expertise and authority is never more evident than when the two search engine results are compared. So, you need to be concerned with Google. And Google has an advertising program that is available for everyone to use. It can cause you huge problems. And it can be used to your advantage.

Google survives and thrives by converting search traffic into money. The process is known as "monetizing traffic." The predominant method by which this is done is AdWords, which is the online advertising vehicle that presents all those "sponsored ads" on the right side, and sometimes just above, the "natural" or "organic" results that evidence the attacks. AdWords advertisements play an important role in reputation management and also online attacks.

As I mentioned, Sue has told the story of her attacker buying AdWords advertisements and having them presented whenever Sue Scheff or PURE is searched. The ad is misleading and causes people to click on the ad thinking they will find Sue, but instead are directed to her attacker's site. Suffice it to say that if this is happening to you, Google won't necessarily pull down the advertisement. This is a complex arena implicating trademark law, contract law, fair use, and free speech.

AdWords advertising is another powerful weapon in the arsenal for attackers and, fortunately, for victims as well. Google attack ads are particularly impactful. If enough money is bid for the ad position, it will likely be presented not on the right side of results, but at the very first position of all search results. Despite a small disclaimer that the ads are "sponsored results," many people don't really know that these are placed advertisements. And even if they do, with a catchy headline it is going to be seen and read.

A title such as "Is XYZ company a scam?" or "The truth about XYZ company" gets attention and is likely going to affect reputation or brand even if the ad is not clicked on, and will often divert a searcher to an attack website. Another common approach for an attacker is to buy an AdWords advertisement with the title "XYZ Company," offer a neutral description in the ad, and then deceptively lure those searching for the attacker's target to an attack website. The most sophisticated ads appear as if they are "XYZ Company" ads, but the site impersonates the company in a disparaging way. I've seen sites with horrible grammar or clearly absurd claims that purport to be the official site of the target, which itself raises a new arena for the courts in interpreting whether this would be defamation.

You can imagine the effect on someone doing due diligence. Confusion, at a minimum, is certain. And confusion on the web means that it is easier to just move on to another applicant under consideration or go to the next business selling a similar product. Confusion on the web is deadly to an online business.

I mentioned that AdWords can be used by a victim. Taking an ad out for yourself when you or your business is searched is essential. You can get the first word in and make the first impression. These ads can be crafted for branding purposes in which you do not need anyone to click on the ad in order to get your position first in line. "XYZ Voted Best Site," or "XYZ Customer Satisfaction Highest," or "XYZ Wins Public Service Award" all send the message of credibility and acceptance and puts all the negative commentary that's to come in the natural or organic results into question. Some businesses have even gone to attacking the attacker in these ads.

Knowing that the first page of Google results carries a particularly effective and false attack on your business, you may want to run an AdWords advertisement that is defensive in nature. "The Truth about xxxx (your attacker)," which leads to a page explaining the attack on your terms. When well done, it can take the sting out of an otherwise deadly derogatory result. And there have been some even more creative uses lately. A particular business under attack bought AdWords advertising that made its ads look like attack ads. "Find the Truth about XYZ" and "Is XYZ a Scam?" could be examples of the type of ad titles it ran. When inquiring minds clicked on the ads, they led to a high quality legitimization of the company, leading everyone to conclude that they had found "the truth," and XYZ was not "a scam." Links then led the visitor directly to "XYZ" company's main e-commerce site.

Note that not only does this type of ad divert the searchers, but it moves them away from returning to the organic results since it conveniently offers links directly to their intended destination. I expect the next generation of this technique will be to offer discounts to those who purchase by going directly from this page to XYZ's e-commerce website. Also note the strategy . . . to get the eyeballs away from Google search results and keep them from returning. This is an ingenious strategy, but one fraught with legal issues that could implicate Federal Trade Commission enforced false advertising laws. Be very careful with this type of a tactic because you could be liable for false advertising.

I would be remiss if the age-old problem of "click fraud" was not discussed. Yes, those attacking you or your business can, and will, click on your pay-per-click ("PPC") ads and basically steal money from you. If you are using PPC advertising, you understand that you pay every time your advertisement is clicked on. So, what happens if someone who does not like you decides to click on your ad over and over again? You have to pay for the ads. And this happens all the time. I have seen discussions on forums encouraging everyone to click on advertisements of a business as part of a mobosphere attack. The good news is that the advertisers, like Google, have very advanced programs to detect these click attacks, but there are many ways to execute such an attack in a stealth manner and not be detected. There are also businesses that can monitor your PPC ads, identify fraudulent clicks, and go to Google and get your money back. This illegal "click fraud" tactic is probably larceny or theft by trick, and, depending upon the amount of fraud involved, could get the clicker charged with a felony. Don't even think about doing this as a defensive move to attack Google ads coming from an attacker. The illegal tricks can be used against you, but you can't use them against your attackers. And attackers may be outside the jurisdiction of United States laws and have nothing to lose.

Isn't it interesting that we allow our laws to be used, and abused, by scofflaws located all over the world? Consider the anonymity issue. Who says that some Russian hacker or Iranian spammer should have the benefit of our free speech, our First Amendment, and the traditions of anonymity practiced by our forefathers? So when you discover who is anonymously running an attack advertisement, expect the issue of anonymous free speech to be invoked to protect everyone in the world.

Section 230's Impact

How can all these sites and webhosts refuse to change offensive and often illegal content? Life would have been easier for Sue if she could just go to the website or webhost, point out the defamatory statements, and have the sites remove the posts. But, as we have seen, there is a federal law that gives them immunity as long as the site doesn't start substantively editing. Think about the implications of such a law and you can quickly see the problem.

What happens if we give legal immunity to the owner of your local newspaper whenever false information is reported? You end up with tabloid journalism at best. Outright lies become a common occurrence. As you get up every morning and start reading the paper a sense of relief washes over as you realize you are not the target of the week. Then you read all about the latest gossip, of course presented as fact. And that would be very damaging or hurtful to someone who didn't deserve it in the least.

You would think we, as a society, wouldn't stand for that. But we do. We accept this practice as a way of life on the Internet. And there is nothing we can do about it until the law changes or the courts continue eroding its impact. Even the local police have no control. A sheriff in a small town called me during the election cycle and had quite a story to tell.

Imagine it's been your dream to start a website with a small "forum" for you and your friends to discuss the annual garden tour and other local civic news in your hometown. For a while, it is a wonderful online community you are building. Advice flows freely about how to get rid of that poison ivy, what fertilizer works best on tomatoes, and how to keep those rodents or deer out of the garden. As spring turns to summer, discussion about the best conditioned golf course takes off among the local guys. But as Labor Day passes by, the local sheriff's reelection campaign kicks off. And since your little website and community forum is so well followed, apparent political opponents of the sheriff start posting claims that he protects the local drug trade, is an active participant in a local gambling racket, and promotes promiscuity. The real truth is that he circles the local pharmacy on his rounds each night, got in on the NCAA tournament basketball pool, and was a judge at the local country club for the annual belly flopper contest on Independence Day. And he runs a tight, tight ship over at the jail.

All you wanted was a civil online community. Now you have created a battleground that is getting you funny stares at the grocery store and snide comments outside of church. Other anonymous posters claim you are supporting the sheriff and start attacking you, and then your forum explodes with comments flying back and forth with all kinds of outrageous claims centering on the character of the political candidates.

The sheriff wanted to know what to do. Why can't the owner of this website be required to pull down all these lies? Well, Sheriff, I replied, because the law requires she not remove any of the posts or she may become a content provider and lose her immunity. She's only following the law, a concept I was sure he would immediately appreciate. I went on to explain that if she edits the posts, she loses immunity and can be sued as if she is a newspaper publisher. Every lie told would then create virtually unlimited financial consequence to her.

I've already discussed how Section 230 of the Communications Decency Act gave the owners of websites on which other people post comments complete immunity as long as they don't substantively edit the content within certain parameters. And if they do edit, they lose the immunity. The people at the controls—with the ability to help regulate the Internet through self-policing by exercising good judgment and promoting civil conduct—have their hands tied. Recall that this law ended up promoting more defamatory and outrageous content. The law of unintended consequences rears its ugly head again. And that is why Sue was so helpless in generating online assistance from service providers throughout her ordeal.

We had another client, a lawyer in a major law firm, who in 1994, at the very infancy of the web, went online and posted some rather choice comments after a night at his fraternity house. Now these comments were showing up out of nowhere after a dozen years. Comments on the web are destined to remain, in one form or another, for posterity. Posterity is a long time. And those comments usually visit at the most inopportune times. Like when you are a lawyer applying for admission to the Supreme Court of the United States. Ouch. Fortunately, the lawyer on the other side understood our argument that his client had not acquired license rights in the content when the prior company that ran the forums had been bought, and he had a peg to hang his hat on. The problem disappeared.

But Mr. Sheriff is not so lucky. He'll likely have these comments show up when his legacy is researched by his great grandkids at the turn of the 22nd century. But I did suggest that, if he wanted to avoid any future problems at election time, he may want to take Internet access away from the inmates over at his tightly run jail.

We'll be discussing this law in more detail when I explain what Congress and the courts can do to really make the web safer for everyone overnight. For now, website owners are handcuffed tighter than a cat burglar caught in an exhaust duct. At least that's the way the sheriff so artfully paraphrased the dilemma Congress gratefully bestowed upon all of us.

NO MAN IS AN ISLAND

The Stranded Are Legion

If Congress would only lend an ear, this is what they need to hear: As isolated and alone as anyone who is a victim of Internet defamation or cyberstalking might feel, one thing I have learned is that this is an awfully crowded island. The one-man canoes, kayaks, and floundering swimmers washing up on shore could fill every luxury cruise ship afloat and more room would still be needed for those lining up by the month, the day, the hour.

I have received countless e-mails from around the world with their senders screaming, "Help me, please! I have nowhere else to turn!" I don't have a website devoted to other victims of Internet defamation, but these desperate souls are doing online searches as they seek out any means possible to deal with a totally unexpected and dire situation that has spun out of their control. My name keeps coming up on such searches due to all the written attention my trial, and its outcome, have received. But there are many people whose distrust of the Internet is so complete, they are afraid to send an e-mail. They call me on my business line instead. Within seconds I know this is not a frantic parent in search of help for their troubled teen, but an adult whose own trauma runs deep. They are so hungry to connect with another human being who might understand what they're going through, they take the chance of calling my office in the hope that *someone* will respond after one too many doors have slammed in their disbelieving faces.

These phone calls, these e-mails, are driven by desperation. I am a last resort, and for anyone to get pushed so far into a corner they've got nowhere else to turn beyond me is almost beyond comprehension—and so, so wrong. That's why I read these e-mails; why I take these phone calls. Because I understand that what other victims of Internet abuse want more than anything is to be reassured that as isolated and repellant as they feel, *they are not alone.*

I think you have to walk a mile in those shoes to completely grasp the intensity of desertion and despair that those of us who have lived it feel. Feel it we do, from the time we wake up till we call it a night. And even in that small respite from reality, nightmares are inclined to intrude. It's almost as if we're members of an elite club that we were all forced to join despite the fact none of us wants to snag a badge or learn a secret handshake to recognize a sorority sister or fraternity bro. And yet once you've gone through the hazing that entitles you to join the ranks of your mutually damaged peers, come what may, through thick and thin, you're all in it together.

I can't tell the stories that have been shared with me nearly as well as those who have lived them. It's hard to choose, there are so many, but here is a sampling (with personally identifying details removed) of the e-mails I continue to receive, seemingly without end:

Dear Sue:

"I've been the victim of Internet defamation for the last two and a half years and have not been able to stop this person from continually writing untrue and very damaging things about me. My husband has also been the target and the things this person has said about him are unfounded and untrue. Of course this comes from an angry and bitter former spouse, who has been asked to stop but still continues to post lies about us and our lives. I have a business and my husband is well known in our community and my fear is that at some point these lies will do harm to both of us.

I've yet to find an attorney in our area willing to take on such a task or one who even has a limited understanding of what to do in such a case. Our state seems very archaic in the knowledge of Internet harassment and defamation matters. Until I married my husband I'd never been a victim of the Internet. We are both very private people and we've tried to quietly end the disputes between his former spouse and us, but nothing has worked. He has children with this person, and it has now come to a point where they are being damaged mentally by the constant interrogation their mother places upon them after they have visited us. This has taken such a hard toll on my health that I now clench my jaw so tight I've cracked teeth and suffer from chronic headaches. I'm at my wit's end so to speak because nothing we've done works. If you, or anyone, could help with a direction to go or a specific attorney to contact, we would really be grateful. Thank you so much for just reading this message. . . ."

Greetings from Canada!

"I see that you are an advocate for those being defamed and slandered online. There is a website that is damaging our business. The content is after the fact and the poster knows or ought to know that the posted information was previously shown to be unsubstantiated, unwarranted, with no grounds whatsoever. Just lies.

The website does not offer any contact information or show any identification as to the poster's identity. I tried to find their IP address but they have somehow blocked this information. I realize our company is in Canada but perhaps your lawyers have an associate they could suggest? I would greatly appreciate your help in this matter.

Best Regards. . . ."

Dear Ms. Scheff,

"I am in desperate need of help. I am a TV star from [redacted], and I and my child are being slandered, harassed, and stalked on the Internet. This woman has posted the most embarrassing rumors and vulgar profanities about both my daughter and I. She has an account on YouTube that has been closed three times for her profanities about me, and now she is posting comments on [redacted]. She says I've been arrested for drugs, I'm a whore, and the FBI busted me for running a sweatshop. I have lost so many nights sleep over this awful nightmare that won't stop. Please help me!!! . . ."

Hi Sue,

"I've been doing some research on this subject, and found your website. Long story short, my husband and I live in a small town and he is the high school principal. Need I say more? We have endured years of abuse from several local websites; is there anything we can possibly do about it? My husband is a great man, neither of us perfect, but we are hard-working individuals. There are also political ties that help fuel these websites' energy. My goal is to do anything I can to hold website owners responsible. My husband believes that ignoring the attacks is all we can do. I hope you can say that we can do more. I am sick and tired of being dragged through the mud. It's hurtful, for not only me, but my family as well. I hope to hear from you. Best wishes in all you do. . . ."

Dear Ms. Scheff,

"My son alerted me that he was one of dozens of his peers who received a defamatory e-mail about me stating that I am a sexual molester, which I am not. Neither do I have an arrest or criminal record for anything. My son defended my honor verbally since he knows his dad is not a criminal.

Many of the boys' parents were alerted by the recipients about the false statements and the rumor mill went out of control. This e-mail led to my dismissal as a teacher, a long-term career ended.

My family attorney stated that this was defamation per se since she knows I am not guilty. She is not a defamation attorney however. I am preparing to sell my home to help pay living expenses. This has been very difficult on us.

I know that you do not provide legal advice. But, I know you have been successful in fighting vicious harmful language on the Net. Can you provide any guidance for my sons and me? Thank you for reading my note. . . ."

Dear Sue,

"I am being accused of some things that I have not done. Some cyber bullies have made up all kinds of lies about me and the website owner won't take them off so the mean and false accusations about me just keep getting worse.

This is all affecting me greatly. I am now in a full blown depression, I can't sleep at night, I am losing time at work because of falling asleep, and I am a nervous wreck. How on earth do I clear my good name? I have tried to ignore it all, and that didn't work. I tried to post one blog, stating that I have not done any of these things, and that made them angrier! I can't win it seems, no matter what I do. . . .

Can you please help? I honestly don't know how much more of this I can take. Thank you SO much. . . ."

Dear Sue Scheff,

"My name is [redacted]. Google me. You'll see why I'm writing. The first link that you see is the work of someone who has been aggressively harassing my husband and I for several months now, since our decision to remove her from our lives. She didn't take it well. The police can't help, because she is not contacting us directly. I just wonder if there will ever be an end, and how can we ever repair our names?

My husband teaches [redacted] on the side to supplement our income and I made his business cards today with no name on them, scared that someone would Google him. We are both so afraid to tell people our names even as we're trying to grow a new business to keep our heads above water. The website with the inflammatory postings will not remove them. What can we do? I am at a loss. . . ."

Dear Sue,

"My husband is the General Manager of a [redacted]. He has been there about 25 yrs. There is a group of people that are trying to get him fired. They write outrageous lies about my husband on their website, but don't sign their real names. This is very complicated, but it is destroying our family. My husband is so stressed that I worry about him having a heart attack or stroke (myself also). Our grandchild lives with us and it has also upset him. He is a cancer survivor and has been through so much, and now this!

These problems are causing us unbelievable stress and depression. My husband is the hardest working, most honest and dedicated person you could ever meet. He doesn't deserve this. I saw you on *The Rachael Ray Show* and wonder if you have any suggestions. We have talked to attorneys and they just say if you are a public figure, people can say anything they want about you. Thank you for any advice you can provide."

And just who are all of these people? They are you and me. A teacher. A principal. A general manager. A nurse. A small business owner. A stepmom. A secretary. A TV personality with a child under attack.

And then, there's another individual who generously agreed to share his story when I asked him to write a little about it. He perfectly captures the insanity and injustice that provides the framework which supports anyone's ability to launch an attack and ruin a life . . . just because they can:

"I am a landscape architect and was consulting on a project. I am not a contractor and do not hire people, but the electrician that I suggested for this customer to interview for the outdoor lighting did a less than acceptable job. The customer would not let him repair his work and in the end blamed me somehow. She loved everything I professionally suggested but decided to go after me personally instead for someone else's work. No one can even speculate any logical reason for her overall abnormal behavior but she became a living nightmare for me.

She somehow found a website that would allow her to cause great harm for someone else's life. She started unloading on me for everything that seemed unhappy and wrong in her own life. She started writing terrible and slanderous and defamatory remarks about my health, my relationships, my wife, and my motives as a person in business. She freely admitted that she wanted to desperately hurt me personally and physically.

After suffering defamation and slander through a simple click on a computer, my life was stolen from me. I have suffered loss in my profession, my health, my right to freely earn a living, my self-esteem, my privacy, personal relationships, community standing, and my overall freedom. This woman (and the enemies she recruited against me) have caused great calculated fears and abuse. With the use of the Internet they became judge, jury, and executioner . . . with no apparent way to appeal.

It feels like someone just gave them a loaded gun. No one can comprehend the devastation this has caused. You are left hopeless with nowhere to turn. How do you explain this public humiliation to your grandchildren, friends, and family? You become a prisoner in your own skin not knowing who has seen this slander and who has not. How do you stand in your local grocery line, post office, or even Starbucks? The fear of all of the above just never stops and they just keep writing . . . and no one stops them! Where is justice?"

Where is justice? A very good question.

I could fill a book, probably two, with more letters like this. Do I get some "out there" correspondence that suggests the sender is either unstable or is likely fabricating a story? Sure I do—but not often. The vast majority of e-mail and phone calls I receive on my business line are filled with honest pleas and raw emotion. These are flesh-and-blood people whose pain, despair, and sense of isolation are very real to me. I have felt what they feel. I still do. These aren't just distressed voices on the other end of a phone line calling a stranger they found on the Internet, or meaningless words transmitted from one e-mail address to the other because the writer has nothing better to do.

These are my brothers and sisters, from small towns to epicenters that are bound together in a net of injustice, so desperate for some contact outside of their isolation that they have reached out to me because they have nowhere else to go. They are trapped without warning in a very frightening place where they don't belong: A leper colony: Population One.

Monkeys don't fly. As much as I would love to believe it, tell that to the Scarecrow fighting with straw arms and getting plucked apart by an army of swooping, screeching animals with half-human characteristics, at the command of a morally impaired and maniacally brilliant source.

Tell that to Megan Meier—only you can't because she's dead. Maybe you remember her from all the news coverage her suicide received once it came out that this emotionally fragile young teenager hung herself after the mother of a friend she had a falling out with decided to set up a MySpace account and pose as "Josh Evans"—a fictional sixteen-year-old who wooed Megan then dumped her in the most malicious of ways.

Fortunately, *very fortunately*, not all teens cruelly baited on the Internet end up as tragically as Megan. I met one such survivor of teenage cyberbullying on *The Rachael Ray Show*, and if I could pick a single character from Oz who best embodies this impressive young woman, it would easily be Dorothy. She's the youngest of all the

characters but wise beyond her years. Life's disappointments, hard-
ships, and wonders have molded her into the strong, unforgettable
character that she is. So, too, with Krysten Moore, 2007 Miss Teen
New Jersey International and a national spokesperson for teen bullying and cyberbullying prevention with Love Our Children USA
(www.loveourchildrenusa.org).

Krysten is an honor student, now in college, who has accumulated
over 7,000 hours of community service, including hospital volunteer
work, the *Jerry Lewis MDA Telethon*, a children's camp for cancer, Habi-
tat for Humanity, the Muscular Dystrophy Association, and is the
founder of Students Helping Instill New Esteem (SHINE).Beautiful
inside and out, Krysten took second place in the national Glamour
Shots Model Search contest, and was a special presenter at the Third
Annual New York State Cyber Security Awareness Conference.
Despite her hectic schedule, when I contacted Krysten and asked if
she might like to contribute some of her thoughts to this book, she
graciously sent me the following e-mail in response:

From: Krysten Moore
Sent: March 04
To: Sue Scheff

Dear Sue:
   Below is a short version of my story. Cyberbullying has become
such a widespread terror and needs to be stopped before it gets
worse. As you know the youth of today is especially vulnerable
due to the marvels of modern technology. I wish you all the best in
your quest to educate others about this societal problem that is no

respecter of age, color, gender, or religious creed. Best of luck and take care.

—*Krysten Moore*

My story began seven years ago when I was in 6th grade. I stood approximately 5'2" and weighed in at 140 lbs, making me a prime subject for my classmates' entertainment. Through my middle school experience I was bullied via the Internet as well as traditional bullying. The cafeteria became a battlefield as horrific remarks like "Krysten wants MOORE food" and "Move it whale" were shot my way; and lockers soon became landing pads as I was shoved in the hall.

But in case school bullying wasn't enough to terrify me, my middle school bullies took it to the next level and became inescapable when they moved beyond the school grounds to the privacy of my own home. The attacks that once had subsided with the ringing of the final bell at 3:00 PM suddenly turned into people posing online as a boy who liked me, only to make fun of our conversation the next day in school. Websites were created posting false and crude remarks about me, slowly diminishing my confidence. I felt as if everyone was against me and that I had nowhere to turn. There was never a night where tears didn't fall from my eyes or that I wouldn't sit in my mother's lap feeling helpless. I knew I had done nothing to deserve the way I was being treated and that something needed to be done.

After many long talks with my parents, I came to realize that the bullies did not define who I was, they defined who they were. I decided that I was going to overcome this ordeal and not let a bully weaken me. I knew it would not be a simple task and that it would take a while. I started my "quest for self worth" by the very same device that had degraded me: The Internet. I researched and read articles from many different sources, most of them saying very similar things. "Don't get upset in front of them," "Stand up to a bully," "It's not my fault," "No one deserves to be bullied," etc.

I can't say that there was an "Ah-Ha Moment" that changed my life, but over the following two years, my confidence grew and my body shrank. Perhaps it was maturity, perhaps it was coincidence, but definitely it was knowledge. Arming myself with the information and suggestions I found on how to handle a bully, robbed them of the power they mistakenly thought they had and placed it in my hands.

Also through the Internet I found Love Our Children USA, the national nonprofit leader in breaking the cycle of violence against children. Teaming with them as a National Spokesperson, I began my crusade about childhood bullying. I have spoken to thousands of elementary and middle school children in the tri-state area, encouraging them to place the same importance on being respect-ful as they do on being great athletes.

Bullying has been around for a really long time, but that doesn't mean it has to exist forever. Whether it's happening to me or you, WE have the power to stop it . . . one positive word at a time.

Krysten speaks eloquently on behalf of the growing epidemic of tortured teens that get bashed because they don't talk right, don't look right, don't hang out with the popular crowd, or don't wear the right name-brand clothes. Any one of these differences makes a good kid easy pickings for those who aren't so good themselves.

When I was Krysten's age, bullying usually took place in clear sight on a playground, or in the form of being publicly ostracized. Say you wanted to eat with someone at lunch, and if you dared to take the one seat available with the "in crowd," then they either ignored you, told you to move it, or made the biggest statement of all by getting up in unison and leaving you there, alone, isolated, a loner who didn't even have enough loser friends to sit with instead.

Clearly, the mean kids are still out there, and some of them are old enough to be grandparents, if not older. As for the cafeteria, easy targets get pelted with whatever can be hurled from a virtual food tray, with no authority figure in sight to demand order and send the deliberately cruel and guilty to detention.

What's sad to me is that some adults who were no doubt mistreated in their youth have the ability to show such a lack of compassion to their fellow travelers in life as they fling poisonous arrows with the stroke of a key, taking cover behind a computer screen as they make a mockery of our precious free-speech rights and wear the camouflage of anonymity.

Come out, come out, wherever you are! But no, that's not how the Internet works. At least not with the laws that are presently in place. That is why something *must* be done to significantly change our virtual-reality playground rules, so the bullies are no longer allowed to call the shots and justice for their victims finally prevails.

It's the End of the World as We Know It

Teach the Children

I hear these stories every day, day in and day out. They are heart wrenching. I often wonder where we, as a society, have gone wrong. While many attacks don't involve our youth, many do.

I was watching a public television program on polar bears. In the spring of each year, as the days become longer, as the streams rage from melting snow packs, and as the first sprigs that by mid-summer will turn desolate ground into meadows teaming with wildlife shoot up, mama bear and her cubs leave the den to venture out into the wilderness. This is a time for teaching and learning. As mother goes about her routine of hunting seals and ground squirrels, her two youngsters watch intently at first, and then begin copying her. No, they aren't going to become hunters and gatherers overnight, but the lessons they learn will soon enough serve them well, allow them to find nourishment, grow up, and contribute to nature's evolution.

Mother bear knows how to avoid the cliffs and maintain a vigilant eye for the threat of wolves. Her sense of smell leads her to sustenance. Her instincts protect her cubs from predatory brothers and sisters who don't mind feasting on their blood relatives and neighborly bear friends.

It likely sounds very familiar to parents of today. Whether by mom or dad or both, we were taught from our infancy by example. And over time we acquired the knowledge to navigate a slippery slope, the instinct to maintain a safe distance from predators, and the motivation and purpose to fend for ourselves. We learned from our parents and followed their examples, albeit begrudgingly. Our parents had learned from their parents. It was all quite habit-forming, actually. Second nature.

But can we, as parents, do the same? Can we really teach our children? The forces at work today shaping their cognitive functions are foreign to us. If they aren't in the living room playing a war game with someone from a country legitimately at war, they are getting married at age fourteen in a virtual world. In between posting their latest photo on Facebook and MySpace, they are uploading their latest cell phone video to YouTube, after which they are tweeting away and playing some video game while responding to text messages. Needless to say, the days of playing capture the flag in the yard, adding extra candy hearts to that very special Valentine's Day card, paging through the family photo album, and chatting away on the only phone in the house are long gone. While the lessons we yearn to teach our children remain the same, the communications platform and information distribution system is passing us by. Our children, and the children of our children, will be the moral compass of the online world. And that is a big part of the problem.

Here's a simple proposal. Parents, if you cannot use and understand the technology your kids are using, then don't allow them to use it. Period.

Top Ten Steps You Can Take Today to Protect Yourself Online

Top SEO Tactics

Ready to protect yourself? Okay, let's get started.

You've seen the late-night infomercials promising real estate riches. I'm going to tell you how to gerrymander your way to real estate dominance . . . but with the virtual gerrymandering of online real estate positions. Google is the leading search engine. But what makes it so? Popularity is the main reason, coupled with trust by the users in Google's judgment. Given Google's prominent mindshare and dominant market share, this won't be changing anytime soon. Before exploring how you can use Google to protect yourself against online attacks, it is worthwhile to understand what Google really does.

Basically, the search engine ranks websites on its opinion of the "authority" of web pages by determining the popularity of a site and the relevance to a particular search. Google identifies relevance by the location and repetition of a term in relation to a web page. When someone searches for "Los Angeles Plastic Surgeon," the site that has the term as its domain name, page title, meta description, HTML headers (use your favorite search engine to learn all about these), and just the right number of strategically placed repetitive uses of the phrase on its page, may be seen as most relevant. The popularity of a site is defined in part by the number of visitors and page visits and time on the site per visitor, but the primary factor is the number of links from other "authoritative" websites to it. Links to a site are seen as a vote for the site by the online public. Mix popularity in with relevance and you end up with the Google "authority." It's much more complex than this and is based upon mathematical equations and algorithms that are constantly being massaged, but you get the idea.

The problem is that "authority" in the eyes of Google is not what most people think. Authority has nothing to do with expertise. It is the product of popularity and relevance. If enough people decide that $1 + 1 = 3$, in Google's eyes it does. Links to a page are a measure not of the popularity of a site as an expert resource, but of the popularity for linking to it. Think of it this way . . . if 1,000 websites were ridiculing a website or online business and linking to it, it is easy to conclude that the site is a popular site to link to, but not a popular site for its authoritative and expert content. In fact, just the opposite is true. The site's content is being ridiculed, not praised. Google doesn't know the difference. So when you search, you are not getting a result determined to really be the most authoritative expert opinion on a matter. The veteran movie critic's review of the Oscar winner has virtually no advantage in Google's "authority" approach over the thoughts of an imaginative sixteen-year-old who offers a seemingly credible review because he was told by his friend that his dad went to the movie and didn't like it.

It doesn't take long to appreciate that Google's challengers for dominance in the online search world will be those who can actually return results based upon true expertise. Of course, this is going to be an interesting battle because the Internet is driven, in great part today, by those pushing the "democratization" of society. In their minds, citizen journalists deserve as much expert recognition as real journalists, law school students as much expertise as judges and prominent jurists, and physical therapists as much recognition and respect as brain surgeons. And Google's approach fits in perfectly with this belief since "authority" is derived, not from a measure of true expertise, but by *mathematical analyses perverted by the ability to manipulate website characteristics and buttressed by perceived democracy in action: a popularity vote of netizens through mathematical link calculations.* The founders of Google were mathematicians, not social scientists. I expect someone will come along soon and figure out how to reliably and objectively evaluate the seemingly subjective factor of expertise, and then the online world will be in for a change, despite the "democratization movement."

Now on to the show! Note the emphasis I have placed on the mathematical calculations and the ability of some to manipulate results? That is what is happening when a Google Bomb goes off, the Streisand Effect is triggered, or someone takes aim at you. The entire focus is on getting negative and derogatory and often defamatory information presented as expert guidance when you are searched on the web. In other words, the Google system can be gamed. And gamed it is. Not only by the miscreants and scofflaws of the world, but by everyone from the Fortune 500 to the stay-at-home mom using search engine optimization and reputation-management strategies, tactics, and procedures. You, too, can manipulate Google results in building up your defenses and responding to online attacks aimed at your reputation and good name.

Over the years Dozier Internet Law has represented search engine optimizers, reputation-management providers, and web developers practicing SEO. We've analyzed all kinds of situations dealing with illegal SEO activities from trademark infringement to copyright infringement, from defamation to privacy violations, and from hacking to outright theft. We constantly review, analyze, evaluate, and recommend courses of action involving SEO issues from both sides of a problem. We even have an in-house "SEO and reputation-management" section of our law firm. But I don't have the room to write, and you understandably don't have the patience to read, an SEO version of *War and Peace.*

So I have gone through and identified some of the most important, easiest, and cost-effective reputation-management steps available. Some of my advice is precautionary in nature, but most of what follows are actions you can take today to start controlling your online reputation. Learn the latest and greatest information about each of these tactics by using Google to search. Remember that you will be presented with the most popular and gerrymandered results, not necessarily thoughts from the top experts.

1. Buy Domain Names:

The overriding concept in acquiring domain names is to consider what can be used against you. We've already identified that domain names containing your name will tell Google that the website is relevant to a search. As a mom or dad interested in protecting your family, buy the .com of all the family names you think others will use in their searches. Hyphens in between the words are seen as spaces to Google, so include the hyphenated versions of the names. Your business will want to acquire its common business name, trademark names, product or service names, and the names of key personnel and executives.

Identify key terms that others would use when searching for you, your family, your business, your products, and your executives. Don't just limit the list to your names. Consider what people would type into Google to find you. For our law firm, our keywords would be our law firm name, website domain name, individual lawyers' names, and terms such as Internet lawyer, defamation lawyer, copyright lawyer, and trademark lawyer. A cool tool to use for this process is Ferret at http://ferret.centralnic.com. It not only gives you bulk information about the availability of different domain names with various extensions, such as .com, .net, and .org, but it tells you who else owns domain names you are searching. Check the owners out, if available, and make sure you don't already have a problem waiting to happen. How many you purchase is driven by your risk, but I suggest buying the .com, .net, and .org if you are located in the United States.

I also recommend you buy up common derogatory terms at the end of your primary .com domain names. Terms like "sucks" and "scam" are common terms used by those launching attack websites against you. Given the many techniques available to use this type of a name in a variety of ways, I wouldn't spend much time on this unless you have a lot to lose. The names usually cost under ten dollars per year. Once you have identified the names you want to purchase, use a search engine to locate a domain name registrar, set up an account, and buy away. I strongly suggest you conduct your own online reputation review and due diligence and select carefully. Understand that some believe the domain name is the number one most powerful reference used by Google in presenting results. That's, of course, debatable, but keep in mind that the one you miss will all too often be the chink in your armor.

2. Build Websites

Some registrars offer free or very low cost websites. They are often easy to set up in a matter of minutes. There are many, many webhosts available that will charge less than ten dollars per month for a pretty nice site. Google gives websites away. Just make every effort to select a vendor who will give you every opportunity to use SEO on your own site. Make sure a Google sitemap is offered for your site or Google may not know you exist. You want to repeat the keyword (the name) you are protecting in the page title, meta tags, headers (particularly header one), and your content (at least three times on your page). Make sure you have the option to do this. Within an hour, you have a website that is optimized, albeit in a very basic sense, for the keyword you are protecting. You can do this again and again and really build up a lot of different websites, all being presented to those searching for you. And it won't be long before they pop up on Google and you start building an online presence that might just thwart some types of attacks and send the scofflaws off to pick on someone else who didn't read this book!

3. Start Blogging

Blogs will be indexed by Google and take up another valuable place on that front page of results. You can start blogging in minutes, for free, at Word-Press.com or Blogger.com. Make sure you use the keyword you are protecting as the name of the blog, and while you cannot optimize a blog on one of these sites like you can a website, at least not without some pretty fancy coding, make sure you use the keyword in the blog title and in the title of every post you make. And you cannot only repeat the keyword in the body of your post, but insert anchored text links pointing back and forth between all of your properties as you build your online defenses. Remember what anchored text links do: they add authority to the page they are pointed to, as well as help your blog relevance, both of which are good for Google results. You now are using the very tactic from which this book takes its name. You are using anchored text links to build up authority so when you are searched on Google your website and blog and other properties will populate prominent positions. You are building a castle. Now let's add a moat.

4. Add a Website Within Your Website

Two sites equal two results on Google. But they both have to work their way up in Google's eyes independently. What if you could add a second website and have it feed off of the strength and authority of your first site? That's free leverage for you. And that's a subdomain. You see them all the time but you probably don't realize what you are looking at. Use your keyword in the name of the subdomain. It will look like http://*dozierinternetlawpc*.cybertri-allawyer.com/. The italicized words (the subdomain) have been added to our law firm domain name (Cybertriallawyer.com) so that the search engines will identify the content in the subdomain as a separate website and return the section as a separate result when our law firm is searched. This subdomain is presently on our law firm's first page of Google results. Of course, make sure you put real content on these subdomains and avoid using duplicate content at all costs since that sets you up for potential penalties from Google. I recommend you do this, if you don't already have a website, using Sites.google.com, the free website portal from Google. The last I checked, they offered free and easy subdomain setup.

5. Go Social Networking

Register on MySpace.com and Facebook.com, but before doing so conduct a Google search about the sites for the term "SMO" (we are now dealing with "social media optimization"), and you will find a wealth of information telling you the latest and most successful techniques for optimizing profiles on these sites. Make sure you research the optimization techniques before signing up since there are some important SEO tactics you should use at registration that cannot be changed in retrospect. Complete the profile and see how it does. This does not require a great commitment of time or a willingness to engage in the social networks on an ongoing basis. But the more you participate the right way, the more SEO benefits will likely accrue. There are also side benefits to doing so . . . you'll be better able to monitor your kids and once they find out you have accounts they'll stay in line. If they are willing to befriend you.

6. Post Pics to Flickr

Consider opening an account on Flickr.com and posting images. You'll find plenty of SMO and SEO guidance online for this site, but the great benefit is that each image is treated like a separate web page that can be optimized. This was reportedly set up like this so that individual images are searchable on Google, which makes sense. What a bonanza. But if you are a business understand that there have been rumblings about Flickr clamping down on business use that is clearly for SEO (okay . . . SMO) purposes with little community interaction. My advice for businesses is to open an account, optimize the images, and then if they perform well in Google results, commit a couple minutes a week for interaction with the community.

7. Sign Up for Everything

Imagine my surprise a couple of years ago when I received an e-mail from our law firm at a Yahoo address. Or my dismay at learning that someone had already claimed our law firm name on a popular blog site. Don't allow this to happen to you. You lose the ability to SEO the exact name you want to protect, and you allow someone to launch a site attacking you or impersonating you. There is a great, free tool available that you should use at www.user-namecheck.com to see if anyone has claimed your name. It covers over sixty websites, including everything from social networks to all the major online e-mail services. All of the sites listed have free memberships. Go register your keywords as accounts on all of them. Some accounts will expire due to inactivity, while others never will. Monitor this on a regular basis and you will have cut off a very popular attack vehicle. Remember the story about the Dalai Lama opening a Twitter.com account? Exactly.

8. Use Personal Branding Sites

Open accounts on LinkedIn.com, Naymz.com, LookupPage.com and Ziggs.com. And most importantly, register a Google profile, which is the recently launched Google personal branding site. You can bet that Google's site will index high in its own results. These sites generate excellent search-engine rankings and are substantive expressions of the real you, often coupled together with your friends' and associates' laudatory praises.

9. Avoid These At All Costs

Never post videos on Youtube.com if you are focused exclusively on personal reputation management. If you are using YouTube as a marketing tool or as a legitimate social networking platform, that's another story. But putting personal videos out there for SEO purposes is dangerous since it might encourage retribution in kind or incite the passion of your attackers once they see your face. And if you hear that Wikipedia is great for SEO purposes because the pages get indexed very high in Google search results, you would be right. But do you mind having a top three Wikipedia search result that has been edited by a bunch of wackos attacking you? I strongly recommend you never, ever consider pitching to open a Wikipedia page. The mantra you should always follow in working on reputation management is to control your content.

10. Investigate the Option of Hiring a Reputation-Management Company

Are you a busy professional short on time? Maybe a little computer challenged? Or feel it's a bit too much work? This option might be something to consider—and if you think the tips in this top ten list are great, you'll be surprised how much more can be done by high quality reputation managers.

There you have it. The blow-by-blow tale of how to turn a little work into riches! More details about outsourcing options are next.

Honey, It's the FBI

Selecting the Right Professional Help

The suggestions I offer on both reputation monitoring (the early warning system) and reputation management (online defenses) are pretty introductory in nature, almost free of cost to you, and not relatively time-consuming. They are also the highest initial paybacks on the investment of your resources. The industry known as reputation management offers extremely sophisticated assistance in a broad arena. These businesses will help you build incoming links to your web properties, which is one of the most important aspects of long-term and sustainable positive Google results. I haven't mentioned the role directories play in SEO or how to build up a stronger presence Google will recognize in social networking environments. I haven't told you about social bookmarking sites or the principles behind blogging for SEO. I could go on and on. That's beyond the scope of this book. But well within the expertise of many reputation-management companies. So, if you are considering getting even more serious about building and maintaining a bullet-proof online reputation (if there is such a thing), here is my guidance.

Sue used ReputationDefender with great success. As she noted, there are many, many excellent reputation-management firms. And if legal action is a consideration, there are some very savvy lawyers to pick from.

Reputation managers (I'll call them the pros) have a strong background in SEO. We already know how important it is to optimize your properties for the Google search engine, and many businesses do just that for sales and marketing. Many of the same principles apply. When you are considering hiring the pros, do your due diligence. Yes, check out their reputation. See if they have been able to get their website rated high for common search terms like "search engine optimization" and "reputation management." If they can't do that, then maybe you should go on to someone else. But don't jump to conclusions. These are highly competitive terms, and this means that any position on the first page of search results is pretty good. First page is usu-ally reserved for the best of the best in the search engine optimization field for obvious reasons.

One rule of thumb is that the higher the result for these search terms, the more expensive the pro. On the other hand, if there is little sign of the pro in the first five pages of results, you should be very careful. There are many, many pros really new to this arena, some who get great results in the short term using "black hat" (unethical) practices that could really hurt you in the long term and others who are high volume, reasonably priced, and will assign you to a lower quality resource within their business. In other words, find out who will be working your account, and understand the makeup of the team. If the pro is not willing to explain in detail what he will do for you, there is a chance it will be "black hat." You can search "black hat SEO" and find out all about these practices that can land you in hot water and destroy your online presence. In other words, do really good due diligence.

About a year ago I received a notice that part of an article on our website had been copied. Imagine my surprise when the impressive website carrying the article was a "reputation-management company" owned by the guy I had just finished suing for fraud and extortion. He was a convicted child predator and real scoundrel running what amounted to a defamation extortion scam against a high-profile client. I called him, and he explained that my article on reputation management was so good he decided to use it in his new business! He took it down when I explained copyright law to him. I think our lawsuit included everything under the sun except copyright infringement, so I am sure he appreciated the free legal guidance. When it showed up again on his site two months later I just shook my head. Yes, it might look like I am endorsing the guy. I realize that. But you have to pick your fights. It's probably still up there today.

Don't have unrealistic expectations. There are several nefarious strategies to get rid of a harmful or negative site. If you are dogged by a forum in which you are falsely labeled a crook or a scam, and it is the second result when you are searched, it will take some real work and time to influence that off of the first page. It can be done by using what I call reverse "black hat" practices. This involves tactics such as replicating the content, getting the new replicated content in place and having the problem penalized ("sandboxed") by Google. Then you have control of the second position and you can start making some changes to your site, and program the changes in such a way that Google does not notice the difference. You could add all kinds of compliments and praise about yourself and bury the negative comments way down the page. This is pure "black hat" and should never be used. Other "black hat" tactics might include purchasing links to your site, or trading links, or hiding text on your pages, or using "doorway pages" that trick Google into thinking the site is one thing when it is another. Just stay away from these. And since these are tactics that are sometimes relied upon by the less than ethical pros, make sure you understand what you are buying. Don't just pay each month for the "magic wand" of the pro. Now I'm not suggesting you ask what Jesus would do, but ask yourself what the public would think. Want to really start an online attack? Play dirty.

There are still CEOs in business who will tell the marketing people to "get rid of this bad search result." That is often not possible. Ethical pros need time to work, and usually six months will be your minimum contractual commitment in retaining a high-quality reputation manager. There is simply no legal way to get rid of a result unless the owner of the site takes it down or a nice webhost decides the site is violating its contract. This will be a very rare occurrence for a number of reasons. Sure, you can hire a virtual hit man to try and hack into the site and stick an ice pick in its forehead or take a baseball bat to its knees. If you don't mind opening your door one day to the FBI. That's neither a pleasant nor inexpensive experience.

Keep it clean. Be careful about who you associate with in this field. And by all means, think long term. There are techniques that will seemingly solve your problems overnight. They are "black hat." There are techniques that can give you quick and impressive results in a short period of time, but they only last a short time. And there are those who offer nothing but false hope. The best thing in the world can be a highly effective reputation manager. And the worst thing in the world can be a highly effective reputation manager. Think process. Not results.

There is some debate as to which comes first, the lawyer or the reputation-management firm. It really depends. But if the time comes for you to consult with a lawyer, here is one piece of invaluable guidance. Check the lawyer out on Google. Keep in mind that a litigation or trial lawyer is constantly in an adversarial role . . . and the lawyer's adversary in a case will often attack the lawyer as a first line of defense. Expect that any experienced trial lawyer handling online defamation cases will, as Sue mentioned about ReputationDefender, undergo online attacks. If there are not any, then you need to ask how aggressive, effective, or experienced the attorney really is. But the main thing you are looking for when you Google the law firm or attorney is its online defenses.

Have they undertaken the basic strategies and tactics I have described above? If not, then the law firm is susceptible to an attack that could, and unfortunately often does, influence the advice and guidance you are receiving. I have seen this happen too many times to count. Your local lawyer writing a "cease and desist" letter is an invitation for disaster. An intellectual property legal expert without defensive positions established on Google is an easy target also. Be careful. And be patient and deliberative in your decisions.

Finally, no matter what options you are considering, gain a full perspective on your options. Don't be afraid even after you have engaged a professional to get a second opinion. If there is any hesitancy to this suggestion by your consultant or lawyer, then a red flag is waving. I am reminded of Dr. Vinny Boombotz, who told Rodney Dangerfield he was going to die. Rodney said he wanted a second opinion. The doctor replied . . . No problem, you're ugly too. That is not the kind of second opinion I am talking about. Sue not only sought expert advice, but decided to carry her efforts a step farther. All the way to the U.S. Congress.

MAPQUESTING THE FUTURE

The Good. The Bad. The Ugly. We've covered them all but I saved a special spot for a beautiful, supportive, and compassionate soul with the kind of clout that can get things done. Thanks to attorney Gloria Pomerantz, doors were opened to give me access to a prominent Florida senator. On October 22, 2007, I had my first meeting with Senator Skip Campbell.

I was surprised to discover that Senator Campbell had a real interest in my story. He was familiar with the lack of legislation concerning the Internet and had been approached by various constituents and personal friends who had experienced Internet vendettas with devastating effects to their businesses and personal reputations.

The fact that he was truly interested and sincerely wanted to help was my first ray of hope that I could somehow contribute to this new era of cyberspace law, and thus intervene, even in some small way, on behalf of countless victims who have been smeared, intimidated, and ultimately terrorized into submission.

A few weeks later, I was contacted again by Senator Campbell. He invited me back for a second meeting. Honestly, when I got that call

I felt as if I was levitating ten feet off the ground. Within thirty minutes of our meeting Senator Campbell catapulted my hopes straight to the sky. He thought this campaign needed to be taken to Washington, D.C. He picked up the phone right then, right there, and called the office of Congresswoman Debbie Wasserman Schultz—and by the end of the day, her office was calling me!

On March 3, 2008, a group meeting took place between Senator Campbell, Congresswoman Wasserman Schultz, my attorney David Pollack, Gloria Pomerantz, and me. We spent an hour discussing the issues of cyberbullying and Internet defamation and at the end of the meeting . . . well, my soaring hopes hit the hard ground of reality.

While the good congresswoman was sympathetic, she likened the situation to President John F. Kennedy's goal of landing a man on the moon by the end of the 1960s, something he expressed in a speech before a joint session of Congress in May of 1961. The Apollo 11 mission made JFK's dream a reality in July of 1969. It took eight years to reach this lofty goal that seemed unimaginable at the time of its inception.

Was Congresswoman Wasserman Schultz implying that the wheels of progress can move slowly, no matter how worthy the quest for advancement and change? Or that a seemingly impossible dream can indeed be accomplished at the speed of light? Whatever her intended meaning, she laid it out straight about the situation as it presently stands: until the Communications Decency Act is updated, there is very little that can be done.

She then invited me to submit some resolutions for potential legislative consideration. Unfortunately, I don't have the legal expertise or political intelligence to accept the invitation, the challenge.

But you know what? I'll just bet that John W. Dozier Jr., Esq., does.

Revolutionary Change

A Call to Action

My goal in this book has been to try and take very complex business, technical, societal, and legal issues and make them understandable. I've learned from the experience, and I hope each of you has too. We've gone through a lot in a short time. I've discussed some solutions to at least part of the problem. And more are upcoming in my final thoughts. I have never been one to dwell on the past or allow the present to define the future, and I hope that you will feel the same way.

Change rarely comes overnight. Changes to big problems don't arise in a vacuum. Great change often evolves slowly over time, a bit here and a bit there, so imperceptible that it becomes unrecognizable in nature. But change it is.

For each of you, I offer this advice: Change at an evolutionary pace will not suffice. Change at a revolutionary pace is the only option. And that revolution starts with each of you. When you teach your kids, please teach them well. I ask you to oppose at every opportunity the decline of civility in society. Have the courage to stand up for what feels right in your heart. But do not ever, ever suffer online scofflaws lightly.

Business Solutions

It's my view that new or amended laws are not the best way of achieving the change that our society needs. But it may be the only way. New legal views and interpretations from judges should be the final frontier to explore. But it may be the only option available. In the rapidly evolving world of the Internet, laws are written that have unintended and unforeseeable consequences. Decisions are made by judges who graduated from law school a decade before the personal computer was invented and commercialized. Our justice system and legislative process are a lot like making sausages. If you knew what ugliness went into the process, you'd shun them forever. But they both are still the best the world has to offer.

So, I offer first my view of how new ideas and concepts and businesses can change the web. And how each of you, viewed together as a society, can make a difference. I'm a veteran of e-commerce businesses. Back in February of 1994 I saw the future and marveled at the possibilities. But no matter how great the technologies might be, the popularity of the web is decided by vote of its citizenry. MySpace, Facebook, and Twitter owe their success to the viral effect of a group hug.

Democratization and Google

What underlying philosophies ruling the web must change? The first is the idea that democratization of everything is good. It is the ultimate equalizer. And in the arena of reputations, it strips the power which society has awarded to leaders and shifts it to the Marxian proletariat. This underlying philosophy is found in the algorithms of Google's search engine. Let the community decide, the mantra insists. Reputations are what the community says they are, the democratization movement believes. But this replaces pure truth with a form of artificiality that suggests there is no truth at all. Truth is a popularity contest. Truth is seen as defined by a homecoming queen contest or a *Survivor* episode. Truth, and through it reputation, is no longer defined by merit.

I trust you are now familiar with Google Bombs. They are the ultimate indicator, in my view, of the damaging impact of a bias toward an egalitarian society. Google defines authority, and therefore presents results under the guise of "authoritative and relevant" resources, based upon popularity. The thirteen-year-old's view could, if the democratization movement elected to do so, be in front of Albert Einstein in Google results as the most authoritative and relevant resource for learning about the principles of relativity. As Google has become the dominant search engine, it has become the reputation engine. But what Google considers worthy of respect and adoration and credibility is far from what most of society thinks. Or what most of society would really turn to in determining someone's reputation. Reputation has become a popular vote of a contrived population, controlled by the misinformed who have the technical prowess to manipulate Google's results and thereby manipulate public opinion. Google reputations are often artificial, fraudulent, contrived, manipulated, and misleading. And the impact continues to grow as netizens no longer seek out a definitive, objective, fair source of expertise and credibility. They just use Google.

But expertise will one day take control of the web and displace the existing Google search philosophies. I don't know if Google will be the one to come up with this change. It seems difficult to reconcile the legitimatization of a bias toward true and honest expertise with the "democratization" movement. But I am equally sure that Google today, as I type this, has a team working on this issue: individuals hand-selected for their "non-democratization" beliefs. We see small businesses coming along that are attempting to create "online merit badges" and "expert passports." The challenge is to establish objective criteria and deemphasize pure popularity as the definition of expertise. The deference and respect shown true experts will then equate into high search results. It will be interesting to see if Google, when this shift occurs, will be leading the pack or just another technology company unable to make the change to a new world order. I can see the day when Google will be the *National Enquirer* of the online world. And ironically, it will be by a vote of each of you. The online society will have voted to leave for greener pastures, tired of the trash Google presents as authoritative.

Self-Policing

Webhosts and payment processors are moving toward "self-policing," the enforcement of performance expectations and rules of conduct laid out in their contracts. This is a very positive development for dealing with online attacks. These businesses are the heroes of the web. They are driving the web toward decency, pulling out miscreants and scofflaws, and throwing them by the wayside. Self-policing must be protected and expanded. General standards and codes of conduct within industries should be encouraged to evolve, although this type of self-policing lags behind the efforts of independent businesses.

These businesses are themselves under attack for trying to self-police and self-regulate by the same groups protecting the scofflaws and thieves of the web. Free-speech fanatics attack the webhosts online whenever a "sucks site" is pulled off the web as a violation of contract. Efforts are underway, for instance, to create a "blacklist" of webhosts that are seen as unfriendly to free speech. On another attack front, a prominent free-speech expansionist and law professor has offered webhosts and other sites preferred language to place into their contracts with customers, which would surreptitiously gut their ability to self-police and self-regulate. The business interests practicing self-regulation are motivated in part by their belief that if they don't clean up their own house a legislative mandate to regulate their industry might do it for them, which would be extremely burdensome. Can the web be trusted to self-police and solve this problem without judicial and legislative intervention? No. And that leaves us with solving this problem through laws.

The E-Bill of Rights

We are facing a unique challenge. Not only are our liberties at stake, but the integrity of the very system we turn to for justice is at serious risk. So the need to deal with online attacks on the good names and reputations of our society's members is pressing. Judges and legislators need to start thinking in terms of "pre-Google" and "post-Google," not "pre-Internet" and "post-Internet." The rise of Google was the defining catalyst for the explosion of reputation attacks. If the Internet is a blasting cap, Google is a nuclear bomb.

With that in mind, let's lay out my proposed "Online E-Bill of Rights."

1. No one shall be required to travel great distance at great expense to seek justice.

In order to bring a lawsuit today against an attacker, you most often have to go to the backyard of the attacker. So if someone is launching one defamatory attack after another from Alaska or Hawaii, and your business is targeted and getting hurt in rural Georgia, the laws, as they exist, require that you travel to the perpetrator's home to file suit and have a jury of the attacker's peers judge your case. This is known as the "minimum contacts" rule. Legislatures need to expand state "long-arm statutes" and courts need to recognize we are now in a "post-Google" era and change the law. You should be able to sue someone in your home state, no matter their home state, if they have targeted you and at the time knew, or should have known, of your geographic location.

2. All shall have the right to seek civil redress from cyberstalkers.

You'll recall my comments about cyberstalking. Congress needs to pass a federal cyberstalking law establishing a civil cause of action as well as criminal liability. States need to change their cyberstalking laws to include a civil version that will create serious economic consequences to those using the web as an assassin's tool. These laws need to have teeth, with statutory damages (like the cybersquatting and copyright laws) and easy thresholds for injunctive relief. And the required element of an imminent fear of bodily harm must be removed.

3. The right to participate without fear in the system of justice shall be preserved.

When a lawsuit is filed against a scofflaw, the mobs often attack the plaintiff.

But that is not enough. So they turn their attacks to the lawyers of the plaintiff. But that is not enough. So the mobs begin attacking the judge, as we have seen. But that is not enough. We have redacted the name of the chairperson of Sue's jury, because next they will come after the jurors. That is why our entire system of justice is so at risk. The rule of law is under attack. Those attacks are against those who dare participate in our administration of justice. And when the mobs decide that jurors . . . and their jobs . . . and their spouses . . . and their children . . . are fair game, are sitting ducks worthy of attention, we are in big trouble. New laws need to be passed to protect the participants in our justice system. Courts need to be more accommodating to allowing plaintiffs to remain anonymous, for court files to be sealed, and for information to be protected from public dissemination. Jury lists and juror names must be protected, and jury-tampering laws must be expanded in definition and scope.

4. The fundamental right to privacy shall be assured.

I have discussed the erosion of the concepts of privacy rights over the past fifty years. State legislators, Congress, and the courts must change the course by recognizing that the invasion of privacy has taken on a new dimension in the "post-Google" era.

5. Anonymity of speakers shall not preclude meaningful access to the courts to seek redress.

Anonymous speech is one of the single biggest problems causing mobospheric attacks. And yet recent court decisions make it more expensive and arduous to sue those who resort to cowardly anonymity to hide their misdeeds. The courts must begin to view anonymous speech as a privilege, not a right.

6. No individual or company shall have its name misappropriated for any financial gain.

There are two problems here. Trademark infringement, the act by which someone uses a business or product or service name to make money in competition with the real owner of the name, usually requires that consumers be confused. If a consumer is not confused, or likely to be confused, there is no trademark infringement. In addition, it is very difficult to get trademark protection for your own name. Scofflaws regularly attack both businesses and individuals and use the attacks to draw traffic to a site, which increases the value of the domain name for resale in the marketplace. They will often add paid links and use other revenue-generating mechanisms. State legislators and Congress need to pass laws protecting names far beyond the existing body of trademark law. Congress and the courts should also begin to recognize an expanded notion of trademark infringement based upon the mere use of a name.

7. Equal legal liability shall attach to every party participating in a mobosphere attack.

It's amazing how we have laws establishing that everyone involved in a criminal enterprise is on the hook for everything done. There are accessories-before-the-fact laws, and accessories-after-the-fact laws, and conspiracy laws. These concepts need to be embraced fully by the civil courts and those participating in mob attacks must be responsible for the damage caused. Otherwise, the mob is motivated to attack even more aggressively because of the difficulty of proving which damages are attributable to a particular element of the attack.

8. The time in which an attack victim must seek redress shall not be limited.

The statute of limitations for defamation is often one year. Yet in the online world, defamation attacks may lay dormant for many years, either through happenstance or by design. Statutes of limitation for online defamation must be repealed by state legislatures. Attackers, once a year has passed from publication, can use SEO tactics to make the defamatory statements visible or can simply remove the "robots.text" code we discussed earlier from the site to make it visible for the first time to search engines. These steps raise the attack to prominence with virtual impunity and immunity.

9. No law shall discourage attack victims from exercising their right of access to the courts.

Several states have passed "Strategic Lawsuit Against Public Participation" (SLAPP) laws, which are one of the biggest threats to the protection of your name. Simply stated, the victim of an attack (when he or she is the plaintiff— i.e., the person who initiates the suit) could be ordered to pay the defendant's legal fees. These laws create an unbearable burden and risk on many victims of online defamation and attacks, and these laws create serious and strong protections for the attacker while the victim is left unavoidably exposed online. If your state has a SLAPP statute, start a movement today to get it repealed by your state legislature.

10. Publisher liability for distributing false and defamatory attacks shall not be abridged.

Of course, the abridgement is already happening. A bit of wishful thinking, perhaps. And I agree that some service providers should not be liable for third-party comments. Given the state of things, my suggestions for amending the Communications Decency Act (a misnomer of monumental proportions) follow:

a. Require those availing themselves of immunity to be bound by an arbitration process much like is done in domain name disputes today.

b. Require retention of complete log files.

c. Establish a "takedown process" whereby a sworn affidavit could be sent to a website disputing the accuracy of information, the poster would be given an opportunity to respond, and rules would govern how to proceed, much like is done today in copyright infringement disputes.

d. Strip immunity from websites publishing anonymous or pseudonymous comments.

e. Establish two classes of service provider immunity; one that applies to ISPs and pure service providers with no ability to alter or edit content, and another class for those who can control content.

These steps will go a long way toward solving the problem.

FINAL THOUGHTS

For myself, I move on from here. I'm an advocate so I move on to every judge who will lend his ear as to why we need to look at a problem in a different way. I move on to the jurors who will one day send messages en masse that will be heard all across our country and around the world. I move on to knocking on the doors of state legislators and asking for better laws. I move on to Congress's chambers and lobbies to push for real laws with real teeth. My message will be clear and strong: We need revolutionary change now. I invite you to join hands to make change happen.

This won't be easy, but since when is anything worth fighting for easy? We'll need your help. Organize locally in your homes and churches and town halls. I have offered my hand of support and guidance. Take my hand. Take my lead. Go to your elected representatives as a group and demand action. Demand laws be passed in your state that will expand "long-arm" personal jurisdiction, create a civil action for cyberstalking, and slap down SLAPP laws. Heck, hand your elected representatives this book and just tell them what you want! Demand that your congressperson not come back home from Washington without a new version of the Communications Decency Act that will assure online decency.

You may have felt helpless as you read our words. How can I protect my children? How can I protect myself, my business, my loved ones? How will I be seen in 100 years in the eyes of my grandchildren? What will my legacy be? What will they say about me and my loved ones when we can no longer defend ourselves? The answer rests in the outstretched fingers of a baby, in the open arms of a toddler, in the hugging embrace of your spouse, in the handshake of your graduate, in the high-five of your buddies, and the interlocking fingers of hands lovingly held. It all starts with an open hand. Some will be extended in support and others surely in need. But our hands will come together as one. Yes, change is coming. With your help.

From: Sue@GoogleBombBook.com
To: You
Date: Today
Subject: Do You Know What Google Is Saying About You?

Victims of Internet defamation reside in a lonely place in our society. My sincere hope is that this book will help you take cover from any threat of a *Google Bomb* launched your way. I encourage you to protect your online image and don't wait until you are offered a spot in my "elite club." Despite the fact that we don't have happy hour here, no tropical mai tais with cute little paper umbrellas in a tall frosty glass, new recruits keep lining up for passage to our island getaway.

Our established membership roster makes it Caribbean clear that Internet defamation is an equal opportunity offender. It does not discriminate on the basis of your profession, sex, color, religion, or anything else that we think might set us apart from every other person in life. From lawyers to landscapers, truck drivers to doctors, teens to grandparents, career women to stay-at-home moms: *NO ONE is immune.*

The malicious stroke of a key has become the equivalent of a cyberbullet. Only it's not just getting fired off into cyberspace, it's hitting intended targets in very real, physical places. The Internet can be a legal, lethal weapon; it can also be a wonderful teaching tool. It's an entity that has taken on a life of its own and must be respected for the enormous power it generates in good and bad, positive and negative, beautiful and gruesome ways. This is the unleashed animal racing through the wild, a sight of awe and wonder—until it turns and sees you, unsuspecting and unarmed against a hungry predator suddenly considering how best to devour its prey. Should it pounce quickly and go immediately for the jugular? Or enjoy a more leisurely meal? As you watch it lick its chops and a pack of its pals circle around you, the anticipation of what's to come next is beyond agony. After all, you know who's being served up for dinner.

This is how it feels to be defenseless against an online attack, singled out and surrounded by a carnivorous foe. I truly believe, I *must* believe, that justice will eventually prevail so that good, decent people can no longer be held hostage by a vindictive ex-spouse, a mentally unbalanced customer, or some acquaintance in class that goes by the name of "anonymous." When justice prevails the afflicted can finally stop looking over their shoulders and no longer be afraid to tell someone their last name or fear for the safety of their job, the continuity of their business, or the salvaging of their house because they just happened to piss the wrong person off.

Unfortunately you can't always know just who it is that wants to maul you to pieces. All you know is that you're frantically dodging a horde of flying monkeys and those cackling witches most wicked. But let us not forget what happened once the mean-spirited hag got doused with some cold water in the face and Dorothy claimed the broomstick that had once been used to terrorize the innocent of the land. *Click, click!* You know the rest. Take care and surf safely! *Sue*

From: John Dozier Jr.
To: You
Date: Today
Subject: Why This Book Needed to Be Written

Creationists believe God built our earth in a matter of days. The Bible's smallest measurement of time is hours. I don't know where the minute gained popularity . . . maybe New York. But when Olympian Michael Phelps took his gold medal by one-hundredth of a second, it was symbolic of the evolution of the importance of ever-decreasing measurements of time. And the speed of change is at the center of the issues we address today.

In the online world, reputations are ruined in nanoseconds. People are branded with a scarlet letter for eternity by someone they don't even know typing away impulsively at a keyboard. The values of business brands, carefully built and shaped over years, decades, and even centuries, are teetering on a precipice of disaster. We are in a world evolving at an ever faster rate. Yet, the families of America, the businesses of America, the legislative bodies of America, and the courts of America lag behind this curve of change. And reputations are being permanently ruined overnight because of it.

Think of it this way. If you grew up in a small town in the South, and the car in front of you didn't take off when the light changed, you learned to patiently wait and even let the light cycle through another time. I love New York City, but if you don't jump on the gas on a green light, the cabby behind you leans on his horn and might give your car a little love tap in the rear as he rolls down his window and flashes his one-fingered peace sign. The online world is the cabby. Society is waiting for the next green light. That's gotta change.

I love America. I love being able to believe what I want to believe. Go wherever I want to go. I cherish the opportunities my children will have as they grow up. And I believe strongly in standing up for what I believe is right and decent. I am sure this is a product of my upbringing. Dad was a Presbyterian minister after earlier careers as a navy pilot and FBI agent. Mom was an intensive-care nurse. Helping people is something that, for me, has been passed down through generations. I'm no measure of my parents, but thanks to them I have a solid foundation. My early years were filled with wonderful memories of character-building events. I remember the time my father went to the front desk of a Holiday Inn and the initial stunned silence of the clerks when he asked if he could pay for a towel to wrap his bathing suit in. "I've never been asked that before," was the response as they thanked him. You know the towels I'm talking about. In fact, you probably had some at home!

I remember the Ku Klux Klan attacks at our house after my father insisted that blacks be allowed to attend an Easter sunrise service on the beach in 1963. I learned all about turning sheets into a rope to escape a fire. I remember the fire in our front yard. I remember Dad's FBI buddies coming into town. And our family having to move north. So, for all of you anonymous hate-mongers, scofflaws, miscreants, and the like who will try to paint my words as some sort of right-wing, un-American, conservative-conspiracy propaganda, I can take it. But also ask yourself if you are any better than the white-hooded cowards who ruled by fire and attacked the defenseless innocent.

For all others interested in creating a more civil, accepting, fair, balanced, and honest online society centered upon good will and fair dealing, my message to you is that you must be willing to stand up and be counted. Hopefully Sue and I have inspired you to action. Moms and dads will begin to take the time to explain to their kids about responsible online behavior. Employers will rule with an iron fist on anticompetitive employee misconduct. The online world will embrace self-policing and self-regulation. The "consumer-rights" organizations will stop supporting the scofflaws of the web. Local, state, and federal legislators will craft laws that establish appropriate mores and norms for online behavior. And the courts will see the need to pull the hoods off of the online scofflaws and expose them to the concept of personal accountability and responsibility.

My message is a call to action. Because time is everything. It's at the core of the problem that we face today. And it's at the core of the solution. There is a time to mourn and a time to dance. A time to cry and a time to laugh. A time to love and a time to hate. A time for war and a time for peace. A time to keep silent and a time to speak.

The time to speak has come.

John

INDEX

ABOUT THE AUTHORS

 John W. Dozier Jr. began practicing law in 1981 and has the highest rating (AV) by Martindale-Hubbell (meaning he has reached the "height of professional excellence and is recognized for the highest levels of skill and integrity"). Mr. Dozier is a "Legal Elite for 2008" as an Intellectual Property Lawyer through a peer selection process of the Virginia Bar Association and *Virginia Business* magazine, was recognized through peer review as a "Super Lawyer" in Internet Law in *Super Lawyers* magazine, was named as one of the top attorneys nationwide for 2008 in Intellectual Property Litigation in the magazine's Law and Politics Corporate Counsel Edition, and is peer selected as preeminent in the 2008 "Bar Register of Preeminent Lawyers." He founded his first venture fund-backed, award-winning e-commerce and Web company in 1994, when there were reportedly less than 1,000 websites in the world. Mr. Dozier is a former President of a statewide specialty Bar Association and the former National Legislative Chairman and Vice President of a National Bar Association, and has testified on e-commerce issues before the United States Senate.

Sue Scheff, founder of Parents' Universal Resource Experts, Inc. (P.U.R.E.), a child and parenting advocacy organization, is often called upon as an expert on Internet defamation by countless mediums after being awarded $11.3 million in a 2006 landmark lawsuit against a woman who posted viral defamatory statements about Scheff and P.U.R.E. She has appeared on *The Rachel Ray Show*, *ABC News 20/20*, *CNN Headline News*, *Fox News*, *CBS Nightly News with Katie Couric*, *CBC Sunday Morning*, and National Public Radio, among others. Scheff lives in Weston, Florida. Visit her at www.suescheff.com and www.googlebombbook.com.